Anonymous

A Historic Discourse:

Delivered at the centennial clelbration of the First Congregational Church

in New Ipswich, October 22, 1860

Anonymous

A Historic Discourse:
Delivered at the centennial clelbration of the First Congregational Church in New Ipswich, October 22, 1860

ISBN/EAN: 9783337820251

Printed in Europe, USA, Canada, Australia, Japan

Cover: Foto ©ninafisch / pixelio.de

More available books at **www.hansebooks.com**

A

HISTORIC DISCOURSE:

DELIVERED AT THE

CENTENNIAL CELEBRATION

OF THE

FIRST CONGREGATIONAL CHURCH

IN

NEW IPSWICH,

OCTOBER 22, 1860,

BY SAMUEL LEE,
Pastor of the Church.

MANCHESTER, N. H.,
AMERICAN STEAM PRINTING WORKS OF GAGE & FARNSWORTH.
1861.

DISCOURSE.

"That search may be made in the book of the records of thy fathers."
Ezra iv : 15.

Reverence for ancestors is natural to man. It is among the germs of character earliest developed, and nearest allied to the religious. To the little child, the parent—first the mother, and after the father—is the object of supreme regard — its Deity. It knows nothing greater, better. Its love and confidence, and obedience and reverence, its adoration, so far as it can be the subject of such a sentiment,—in a word, all that in future years it renders to God, is now bestowed upon the parent. But by and by that child learns that this parent treats as a superior, and loves and reveres his parent; and the child accordingly sends up a higher reverence. And if still another generation be living, the same law of ascent obtains, and the thin and hoary locks of the patriarch inspire a sentiment of adoration profound and sacred.

Thus originated and developed, the sentiment of reverence for ancestors becomes a prominent and influential element in human character. Among all nations, who are so far civilized as to have in any sort a history, early ancestors and the founders of empire are objects of the highest veneration, and sometimes of deification. In the absence of actual excellence, fiction invests them with glory, and presents it in the beauties and the charms of poetry. The early heroes of Greece and Rome are thus glorified and elevated to a sphere above that of mortality—their parentage with the gods, their history superhuman, and their death a deification. And, so that it be regarded as poetry and not history, we object not to the fiction. Its ethical import is good. The natural sentiment of reverence for ancestors finds an object for its regards possessed of an elevating power, and giving to individual and national aspirations a higher aim.

We find this principle of our nature operative in the Jewish nation. Not fictitious, but real were the excellences, worthy of all imitation, in their great Ancestor. And the pen of inspiration ever points to the example of faithful Abraham, as a means of inspiring the faith and prompting the obedience of his posterity. Nor is his influence confined to his natural descendants. In Abraham originated not only the Jewish nation, but the church of God on earth—the spiritual Israel of every age. All who are of faith, are the children of Abraham, and upon them all comes, from this source, a power that assimilates to God. And it will be thus till the end of all things.

To those who have studied the law of divine communications in Christ Jesus, it is a fact full of sacred significance, that the religious element enters so largely into the foundations of our history as a town. The original grant of the township to certain petitioners, inhabitants of Ipswich, Mass., by the Legislature of that State, was essentially religious. It was " ordered that the said town be laid out into sixty-three equal shares, one of which to be for the first settled minister, one for the ministry, and one for the school." Also, " that they settle a learned and orthodox minister, and build a convenient meeting-house for the public worship of God."

When, at a subsequent period, it was decided that the

town, or most of it, fell within the State of New Hampshire, and that therefore the original grant from Massachusetts was null and void, the original Proprietors peti-
tioned the General Court for redress ; and in enumerating
the particulars of expense incurred by them, state that
they have " built a meeting-house."

And when, in 1750, the "Masonian Charter," whose
Centennial we celebrated ten years since, was given, it was
with similar religious conditions. It was required " that
a convenient meeting-house be built in said township
within seven years from this date, as near the centre of
said township, and at such place as the major part of said
grantors and grantees shall determine by vote in Proprietors' meeting, called for that purpose: and that ten acres
of land shall be reserved there for public use ; and that
said grantees shall, within seven years, settle a learned
and orthodox minister in said township, and for whom
suitable provision shall be made."

In accordance with the spirit and design of these grants,
the grantees seem to have conscientiously acted. Previous to the coming in of the settlers under the Massachusetts grant, men were sent forward to erect a temple for
the God of the Pilgrims. The first structure of any kind
reared within the town was for God and his worship.
And when, in the summer of 1738, Abijah Foster came
with his family, and built his cabin on the sunny hill-side
where now is our central village, there was before him, on
the summit of the opposite hill, a house consecrate to the
purposes of religion. God was here first enthroned, and
the way thus prepared for the in-coming of those who
should dwell among these hills and valleys.

Of this first meeting-house, it is said in our town history
that " no evidence or even tradition exists that it was ever
used as a sanctuary." This statement is, however, merely
negative. The house was destroyed by fire during the

absence from the town of the inhabitants, who fled from fear of Indian attacks, in 1748. Previous to this the number of families was indeed very small—not more than twelve or fifteen, it is thought,—and the worship of the Sabbath might have been in private houses. Presumptive evidence of this is supposed to be found in a vote of the Proprietors, October, 1753, " to meet for public worship at the house of Joseph Kidder* for the future,"—implying that they had been in the habit of thus meeting. But they had been without a meeting-house for a period of five years, when, of course, they must have worshiped in private houses.

I know of no positive evidence that the first meeting-house was *not* used for worship. It is a legitimate inference from the character of the first settlers that they had public worship on the Sabbath ; and if so, why should it not be in the house reared for that purpose ? I prefer to believe that it was.

In the year previous to that of the vote to worship in the house of Joseph Kidder, the town had voted to build a meeting-house. This vote, however, was not at once carried into execution. It was not till 1759—seven years after the above vote—that the house was finished and in form appropriated to the worship of God. The house was thirty-two feet by twenty-two, with " nine feet stud." The only finish was that of the external covering. The seats were movable ; some of them denominated " long seats," and others " short seats." Upon these the people were " seated " by a committee, whose business it was to give to each man a place of honor corresponding to his rank in society. And in this house it was that one hundred years ago this day the first pastor was ordained, the church having been organized in it the day before.

---

* Where now stands the house of John Preston, Esq.

The organization of the church—the great fact that has called us together to-day—deserves especial notice.

It would seem, from such a catalogue of the church as we have from various sources been able to prepare, that most of the first settlers of the town were men of religious principle, and either were in form members of the church, or sofar reverenced its institutions as not only to attend and support public worship, but to avail themselves, in behalf of their children, of one of its sacraments, on the principle of the "half-way covenant."

It may be necessary to the younger part of my hearers, to explain what is meant by "The Half-way Covenant." The Pilgrim Fathers attached great importance to baptism. And for about a century previous to the time of which we now speak, the practice had been very extensive in New England for persons who respected religion and its ordinances, but who were not members of the church, to "own the covenant," as it was called, that is, to assent to the covenant of the church as read to them publicly from the pulpit, and as a consequence—though they did not partake of the Lord's Supper—to present their children for the ordinance of baptism. This was called *The Half-way Covenant*. And this was practiced by the church in New Ipswich in the earlier years of its existence.

It would seem that from the earliest practicable period public worship had been observed. In 1750, the second year after the flight and return, provision was made " for preaching in the fall of the year," and a committee was chosen " to provide a proper person to preach." In 1752, it was voted " to have constant preaching hereafter,"—a purpose which it seems was not adhered to, as in 1754, it was voted " to hire two months' preaching in six months next coming, and no more." Who all the persons employed were, we know not. But among them were Rev. Francis Worcester and Rev. Daniel Emerson, both of Hollis.

The first Wednesday in January, 1755, was observed as
" a day of fasting and prayer to God for his directing of
us in the choice of a minister." In February following,
it was voted " to proceed to settle a minister "; and after,
" that Mr. Peter Powers be our gospel minister." In ne-
gotiating with Mr. Powers, a serious difficulty was found
in his dissent from the practice of baptizing infants on the ·
" half-way covenant." This objection was, however, finally
waived, and Mr. Powers in form accepted the call. The
day was fixed for the ordination, and the council invited.
With the council Mr. Powers was not satisfied, and wished
a new and different one invited. The request was denied,
and so the engagement relinquished. The next year, Mr.
Powers was again invited, and with an increased salary ;
but he declined.

In October, 1757, a call was given to a Mr. Deliverance
Smith, which was not accepted.

In the winter of 1758-9, Mr. Stephen Farrar, of Lincoln, Mass., a graduate of Harvard College, a youth of
but twenty years the 8th day of the preceding September,
was hired to preach. After a long probation, he was, in
November following, " chosen to be our gospel minister in
this place." This was not a call from the church, for
there was no church, and was not, therefore, an ecclesiastical procedure. It was given by the Proprietors, for a
town was not yet. But, whatever may be wanting in
form, the call was from honest hearts, and owned and
blessed of God.

The call was accepted the 30th of July following ; and
the ordination took place October 22d. A council was
invited for the two-fold purpose of organizing a church
and ordaining its pastor. The council met Tuesday, the
21st, and on that day gave formal existence to the church,
and on the day following performed the services of ordination—ONE HUNDRED YEARS AGO THIS DAY.

9

The following is the account of the organization of the church, found in the records of the church, and in the hand-writing of Mr. Farrar:

" October 21, 1760.—A council was convened at Newipswich, at the request of the inhabitants, in concurrence with Stephen Farrar, their pastor elect, to countenance and assist them in embodying into a church, and, if the council should think proper, to proceed to the ordination. Accordingly, the following covenant was presented, and after serious prayer and deliberate consultation, with the advice of council, it was unanimously agreed, by those who were members of other churches, and had obtained regular dismissions from them, to unite and embody into a church, by a solemn covenant in the following form—viz.:

WE whose names are hereunto subscribed, inhabitants of Newipswich, so called, acknowledge the great goodness of God to us, both as to outward and spiritual mercies and blessings ; and being, as we apprehend, called of God to enter into the church state of the Gospel, for the free enjoyment of God's worship and ordinances, do, in the First place, acknowledge our great unworthiness to be so highly favoured of the Lord ; at the same time, admiring and adoring the free and rich grace of God, that triumphs over so great unworthiness, with an humble dependance on the grace of God, we would now thankfully lay hold on his covenant, and choose the things that please him.

WE now declare our serious and hearty belief of the Christian religion as contained in the sacred Scriptures, the rule of faith and practice, as it is usually embraced by the faithful, in the Churches of New England, which is summarily exhibited, in the substance of it, in their well known confession of faith. Heartily resolving to conform our lives to the rules of Christ's holy religion, as long as we live in the world ;—

WE give up ourselves to the Lord Jehovah, who is the Father, Son and Holy Spirit, and avouch him this day to be our God—our Father.— our Saviour and our Leader ; and receive him as our portion forever ;—

WE give up ourselves to the blessed Jesus, acknowledging his true *Deity*, and to adhere to him as the Head of his people, in the covenant of grace, and rely upon him as our Prophet, Priest and King, to bring us to eternal blessedness ;—

WE acknowledge our everlasting and indispensible obligations to glorify God, in all the duties of a sober, righteous and godly life ; and more particularly in the duties of a Church state, and a body of people associated for an obedience to him in all the ordinances of the Gospel ; and we thereupon depend on his gracious assistance, for our faithful discharge of the duties thus incumbant on us. And we desire and also promise and engage, with divine assistance, to walk together as a Church of our Lord Jesus Christ, in the faith and order of the Gospel, so far as we do know or shall have the same made known to us—carefully and conscientiously attending the public worship of God and the sacraments of the New Testament; and that we will be observant of the laws of Christ's kingdom which regard the discipline of the Church, as they have in general been administered in the churches in New England, before mentioned ; and that we will attend all God's ordinances and institutions in communion with one another, watching over one another with the spirit of meekness, love and tenderness ; and that we will carefully avoid all sinful stumbling-blocks, strifes and contentions ; and will endeavour to the utmost, to keep the unity of the spirit in the bond of peace.

AND we do now, with ourselves, present and dedicate our offspring unto the Lord, resolving, with the help of divine grace, to do our part, in the method of a religious education, that they may be the Lord's, and that we will carefully keep up family religion.

AND all this we do, flying to ye blood of the everlasting covenant for the pardon of our manifold sins, praying that the Lord Jesus Christ, who is the Head of the Church, and the great Shepherd, would prepare and strengthen us to every good work to do his will, working in us that which is well pleasing in his sight ; to whom be glory forever and ever—   AMEN.

EPHRAIM ADAMS,   STEPHEN FARRAR, *Pastor elect,*
JOSEPH BATES,   STEPHEN ADAMS,
THOS. FLETCHER,   JOHN DUTTON,
ANDREW SPAULDING,   REUBEN KIDDER,
JONAH CROSBY,   EBENEZER BULLARD,
AMOS TAYLOR,   JOSEPH STEVENS,
ZACHERIAH ADAMS,   BENJAMIN HOAR,
                          BENJAMIN ADAMS,
                          THOMAS ADAMS,
                          JOHN CHANDLER,
                          JOSEPH BULLARD."

We have above the names of eighteen persons, including the pastor elect, that were members of other churches, and were now incorporated on the authority of letters of dismission and recommendation. They were of the settlers of the town. Eight of them were original grantees, to whom the Masonian Charter was given.

It would seem that, in accordance with the practice of the early New England churches, a creed of the church was not used in the admission of members, nor was subscription to one required during the ministry of Mr. Farrar. Indeed, it had no creed, except the reference to the Cambridge Platform in the original Covenant, and the incidental avowal in the same, of the doctrines of the Trinity and the Atonement. The following is the form of admission used by the first pastor:

" In the presence of God, his holy angels and this assembly, you declare, so far as you know your own heart, you are serious and sincere in this great act of dedicating yourself to God. You acknowledge the great goodness of God to you, both as to outward and spiritual mercies and blessings ; and being, as you apprehend, called of God to make a publick profession of his name, and to join with his church for the free enjoyment of all gospel ordinances, you do, in the first place, acknowledge your utter unworthiness to be so highly favoured of God ; at the same time, admiring and adoring his free grace, that triumphs over so great unworthiness ; you would now, with a humble dependance on his grace, thankfully lay hold on his covenant and chuse the things which please him.

You do now sincerely and very solemnly give up yourself to the glorious God, who is the father, son and holy Ghost, and receive him as your God and portion, desiring to live unto him.

You do give up yourself to the Lord Jesus Christ, who is God manifest in the flesh, as unto the head of his chosen people in the covenant of grace, and receive him as made of God unto you, wisdom, righteousness, sanctification and redemption.

You do likewise give up yourself unto this church of his, engaging with his help in the communion thereof to attend upon the Ordinances of the Gospel whilst your opportunities to be thereby edified in your most holy faith shall be continued to you.

Do you consent to all this ?

We, then, the Church of our Saviour in this place, do receive you into our sacred fellowship and communion, and promise, by divine assistance, to treat you with such tenderness, affection and watchfulness, as your sacred relation to us now calls for. This we do, implor-

ing of our lord that both we and you may obtain mercy to be faithful
in his covenant, and glorify him with that holiness which becomes his
house for ever—   AMEN."

We cannot suppose that the eighteen persons above
named were all of the settlers who were members of
churches. It will be noticed that they are all males.
Many, doubtless, of their wives, possibly all of them, were
professors of religion. The design of the act of incorpora-
tion was to originate a church as a nucleus around which
all who loved the Lord Jesus Christ might be gathered.

The history of such gathering during the first four years
is entirely wanting. The young pastor, it would seem,
did not keep a record of the church in form till four years
after his ordination.

In 1764 was commenced a record of the church on a
single half sheet of foolscap doubled into octavo. In this,
entries are made under the following captions: "Baptisms," i. e., of infants; "Dismissions from other churches
to this"; "Persons who have owned the Covenant," i. e.,
persons whose children have been baptized under the
"half-way covenant"; "Admissions into the church," and
"Marriages." The entries of this book end in 1773. Of
infant baptisms there are here recorded seventy-nine.
How many of the parents were members of the church,
and how many had only "owned the covenant," we cannot know. Admissions, thirty-eight, of whom thirty-three
were by profession, five by letter; thirty owned the covenant. Marriages, ten couples.

Near the close of his ministry, Mr. Farrar commenced
a record of the church in a volume of ample dimensions,
including "admissions," "dismissions," and "baptisms."
But in this there are no entries under these heads earlier
than 1800. If any official record was kept between 1773
and this date, it is lost.

The blank between 1760 and 1764 we deeply regret. The names of those who were first admitted to the church we would gladly know. There were such, of course. That there were baptisms of infants before 1767—the earliest date under this head—is also to be supposed.

There is a private record of great value from the pen of Dea. Benjamin Adams, entitled "The names of the Church of Christ in New Ipswich, September 19, 1786." First are given the names of ninety-one members, without the dates of their admission. This includes but six of the eighteen original members. February 19th, 1786, one is admitted; March 12th, two; May 7th, fourteen; July 2d, twenty-six; September 3d, thirty-one; November 5th, thirteen,—eighty-seven in all by profession. One this year was received by letter, making a total of eighty-eight. This record of admissions comes down to September 2d, 1803, and laps a little, therefore, upon the official record which Mr. Farrar begun in 1800. Since this date, there is what purports to be an official record, and since 1786 an actual record of admissions.

There is also a private record of admissions to the church by Josiah Walton, from 1786 to 1823. This is imperfect, as we find admissions recorded by Dea. Adams of which Mr. Walton makes no mention.

We return from this digression in explanation of the records of the church.

The next event in order that claims our notice, is the building of a new meeting-house. The present house, thirty-two feet by twenty-two and nine feet stud, was found "too strait." Within three years from the time of its completion, the subject of building a new house was brought forward for the consideration of the Proprietors. The organization of a church and the settlement of a popular pastor, together with other causes of prosperity, had so increased the population of the place, as to suggest this measure.

14

It is unnecessary for me to go into the history of our
meeting houses, as that history has been so thoroughly
written in the elaborate history of the town. Suffice it to
say, that as seven years were spent in controversy between
the commencement and completion of the former house, so
in this instance, true to the prospective character and history of the town, parties in bitter opposition consumed
eight years in conflict. And the location of the house was
decided only by a petition to the Governor, Council, and
House of Representatives of the Province of New Hampshire. A Committee was appointed by the Legislature who
visited the town, and heard the parties, and who reported
to the Legislature in favor of a location for the house.
The report was accepted, and " the Place for Setting the
Meeting House in said Ipswich Established agreeably
thereto." This " Place" was, as my hearers know, directly opposite to the old Burying Ground. The house was
so far finished as to be occupied in 1770. It was 60 feet
by 45, and 26 feet posts. I know of no better method of
presenting to my hearers the house and the times, than
by the following extract from our town history. It is from
the pen of Dr. Gould:

" The old meeting house and the old church-yard are revered objects
in every place ; and as our " old meeting house" is dear to the memory of many persons still living, and may be an object of curiosity to
those of fewer years, a description of it, as it arises to the mind's eye,
together with some of the customs of worship which prevailed during
its days of glory, may not be unwelcome ; and will also be the best
method we can adopt for presenting some of the most important features of the town history.
At the time of its erection it was the largest building within twenty
miles. It stood on the brow of the hill, just north of the old burying
ground, facing the south : and as the land inclined rapidly towards the
east, that end had around it a wharf or wall of uncemented stones
about six feet wide, and nearly as high. This was built in the year
1790. At the north east corner was a large stone which was used as

a horse-block. There was neither tower nor portico; the exterior was never painted, and of course presented the weathered and dusky appearance usual under such circumstances. The windows were small with heavy sashes, and panes of 7 by 9 glass. The doors were single and composed of numerous panels. There were three entrances, one at each end, and one in front, with aisles crossing the center at right angles, and also one surrounding the house next to the wall pews. Opposite to the front door was the pulpit; and in each of the front corners was a flight of stairs leading to the galleries. The posts were very large, extending the whole height of the house, and projecting into the house; towards the top, where they were to receive the beams, they were enlarged, somewhat like the capital of a column. The walls were plastered, though never white-washed; and as they were never tarnished by fires or lights, they maintained a very respectable air of cleanliness. The galleries were lofty, resting on columns about a foot in diameter. The breastwork of the gallery was composed of large panels and ornamented with a heavy cornice. This, together with the posts, was painted of a nameless color, approaching somewhat to poppy red, and grained in imitation of marble or mahogany. There was a row of wall pews, twenty-four in number, surrounding the house both above and below. The body of the house was divided into two portions by the transverse aisle. On the half next the door were twelve square pews, esteemed the best in the house, while on the half next the pulpit were long seats extending on either side, from the broad aisle to the side aisles. They were not like the slender, sloping, sofa-like slips of the present day, but good substantial benches, made of thick plank and capped with good sized joists. The galleries were furnished with similar seats. The pews were occupied by the principal families, while the long seats were free to all, and were occupied by what might be called the common people. Over the stairs, at the south west and south east corners, were the negroes' seats. The pulpit was lofty, and the ascent to it was by a flight of stairs outside, with a balustrade of curiously twisted balusters. It had a recess or rostrum in which the speaker stood; behind him was a curtainless arched window: above him was a curious gilded canopy, about six feet in diameter, resembling in form a turnip cut in two transversely. It was called a sounding-board, and hung near the speaker's head by a slender iron rod from the ceiling, so slender as to have excited apprehensions and speculations in many a youthful mind as to the probability of its falling;—and beneath him, in front of the pulpit, were the deacons' seats, in a sort of pen, where they sat facing the congregation, with the communion table hanging by hinges in front of them. The pews were about six feet square; their walls were high, having also a railing of little balusters around the top; a row of hard, uncushioned seats surrounded the interior, and often there were two or three high-backed flag-bottomed chairs in the center. The seats were hung by hinges, so that they might be turned up, as the congregation rose at prayers, as was the goodly custom of our fathers; and the slam-bang, as they were turned carelessly down again, at the close of prayers, not unlike a volley of musketry, was no inconsiderable episode in the ceremonies.

Behold now the congregation, as it assembles on the Sabbath. Some of them are mounted on horses; the father, with his wife or daughter on a pillion behind him, and perhaps also his little boy astride before him. They ride up to the stone horse-block and dismount. The young men and maidens, when not provided with horses, approach on foot. They have worn their every-day shoes until just before coming in sight, and have there exchanged them for their clean calf-skins or morocco, having deposited the old ones in some unsuspected patch of brakes, or some sly hole in the wall. They carry in hand a rose or a lilac, a pink, a peony or a pond-lily, (and this was the whole catalogue of flowers then known) or what was still more exquisite, a nice bunch of caraway seeds. Instead of this, in winter, they bear a tin foot-stove, containing a little dish of coals which they have carefully brought from home or filled at some neighboring house; and this was all the warmth they were to enjoy during the two long hours of the service. They have come a long distance on ox-sleds, or perhaps have skimmed over the deep, untrodden snow on rackets. They enter the house, stamping the snow from their feet, and tramping along the uncarpeted aisles with their cow-hide boots. Let us enter with them. The wintry blast howls around, and shrieks among the loose clapboards; the half-fastened windows clatter; and the walls re-echo to the thumping of thick boots, as their wearers endeavor to keep up the circulation in their half frozen feet, while clouds of vapor issue from their mouths; and the man of God, as he raises his hands in prayer, must needs protect them with shaggy mittens. So comfortless and cold, it makes one shudder to think of it. In summer, on the contrary, the sun blazes in, unscreened by blind or curtain; the sturdy farmer, accustomed to labor all day in his shirt sleeves, takes the liberty to lay aside his coat in like manner for the more serious employments of the sanctuary; especially is this the case with the singers, who have real work to perform.

Every man is in his appropriate place; for it was little less than sacrilege, in the days when the Sabbath was kept with all Puritan gravity and severity, to stay away from meeting, let the weather bo what it might. See the row of hats hanging upon pegs in front of the gallery. There in the body pews, on the right hand of the broad aisle, are Kidder, Cummings, Fox, Spear and Fletcher ; on the left are Merriam, Barrett, Breed, Moses Tucker and Abijah Smith ; in the large corner pews at the north east and north west are Ephraim Adams and Dix or Batchelder, and between them and the pulpit are Farrar, Benjamin Adams, Nathan Cutter and Eleazar Cummings, Hoar, Start and the minister's pew ; along the eastern side are Knowlton, Appleton and Holden ; along the west wall are Mansfield, Knights, Champney and Hills; and in the front are Brown, Heald, Preston, Spaulding and others. In the western gallery are Walton, Pollard, Bates, Joseph Kidder, Whittemore and Wheat ; in the eastern are Goold, Parker, Cutter, Barr, Robbins and Brooks ; and in the front gallery, Stephen Adams, Francis Fletcher and others. Adams, Appleton and Chandler are in the Deacons' seats ; a goodly band of veterans occupies the long seats below, while the rising generation sits in those in the gallery ; and Patience and Rosanna, and Cæsar and old Boston occupy the negroes' seats.

The prayers are offered ; and during the long prayer, and long indeed it was, a pause is made at a certain stage of it, for those who choose to sit down. The sermon begins, and advances by regular approach up to 8thly and even to 16thly : the elderly men, unaccustomed to long sittings, occasionally standing erect or stretching over the breastwork of the gallery to relieve the fatigue of their position ; Tate and Brady is lined off, two lines at a time, by a person selected for the purpose, and sung with good nasal twang and hearty good will to some good old St. Anns or St. Martins ; and finally, the benediction is pronounced. The congregation still remains in its place to go out in prescribed order : first the minister—and as he passes the deacons they follow—then those in the front seat below, and at the same time those in the front gallery seat and those in the pews—then those in the second seat, and so on in successive order. Would that a like decorum in this respect could be substituted for the impatient and irreverent rush of modern days ! They separate for a short intermission, and to dispatch their lunch of doughnuts or apples ; in summer they stroll in the grave-yard, to hold silent converse with those who sleep there, and impress the lesson of their own mortality ; and in winter those from a distance take refuge before the blazing hearth of some friend in the village, and are perhaps regaled by a hospitable mug of cider ; and soon all are re-assembled for the afternoon service.

c

After this they wend their way home, to partake of a hearty warm dinner, the best of the week, in most instances too, prefaced by an exhilerating draught of hot toddy, and finally to " say the catechism." That Westminster Assembly's Catechism ; who that was trained in the early part of the century shall forget it! Its pictorial alphabet of aphorisms,

'In Adam's fall we sinned all ;'
'My Book and heart shall never part;'

the story of John Rogers ; Agur's Prayer ; and dialogue between Youth, Christ and the Devil ;—it was the only book besides the Bible and Psalm Book allowed in the hands of youth on the Sabbath. The Catechism concluded the religious observance of the day."—pp. 151 —156.

We now have come to one of the most—perhaps the most—interesting period in the history of this town. The elements of religious prosperity are here in marked prominence. A church had been organized, an able and faithful pastor settled, and a meeting-house capacious, and for the day convenient and not inelegant, built. Upon this field of his labors, the pastor, now no longer youthful, laid himself out in true fidelity. And while, before the strong arm of the feller, the forests were retiring and giving place to the precious grains, so under the genial influence of the appropriate means the plants of righteousness were springing up. They did not, indeed, spring up at once. The seed had, some of it, been long scattered, while yet no palpable sign of its germination appeared. And the good man who had preached to this people more than twice or thrice the average length of the pastorates of the present day, was compelled, as he covered his face and wept, to exclaim that he had preached here more than twenty years, and knew not that he had done any good. But this very agony of the pastor's spirit was evidence of the opposite, and showed that the Holy Spirit was making him ready for the reception of rich blessings. And those blessings came.

The winter of 1785–6 is distinguished as the time of the Great Revival. In the earlier part of the writer's ministry in this place, there were several aged members of this church who were the subjects of that revival, and from whom he took much pains to learn minutely the facts of interest that marked the work. A few years ago he was requested by the Author of "New Hampshire Churches" to prepare an account of that revival for that work, and which we will here introduce :

"There seems to have been but one general revival during the ministry of Mr. Farrar. That was such as to merit particular notice. The writer has taken much pains to gather the facts from living witnesses who were the subjects of the work. This revival commenced in the autumn of 1785, and continued through the winter and into the summer following. Of the feelings that preceded the revival, on the part of Christians, little can be learned, as no one who was then such is now among this people. It seems there was less of expectation of a revival than Christians now have learned to entertain ; though there was much tenderness and concern for the souls of men. It should also be remembered that this was a period of great darkness and declension in the New England churches ; being about forty years after the revivals in the days of Edwards, and seven years previous to the revivals which commenced in Connecticut, under Griffin, in 1792 ; and that to the re-action of the excesses of the revivals of 1740, in some respects so glorious, were now added the baleful influences of the Revolution, and of the French infidelity, that came to us with the aid so essential to our armies from that nation. The Christians of that day knew not what a revival was. When it occurred, it was a thing entirely novel. The following incident, witnessed by the person who related it,* though himself at the time an unconverted man, is full of meaning in this connection : About a year before the revival, Mr. Farrar was at the house of his father, who was a member of the church, and conversing with him on the state of religion at the time. In the course of the conversation, Mr. Farrar remarked—'*I have now been more than twenty years in my ministry here, and know not that I have done any good*,' and burst into tears and wept freely. This is significant of what were the feelings of at least the minister,

---

* John Binney.

and probably of some others of the church for a period previous to the outpouring of the Spirit upon the people.

As stated above, the revival began in the fall. The sudden death of a young lady had great effect upon the public mind. In the latter part of December, the solemnity had become very deep and general. On Sabbath preceding the first Wednesday in January, 1786, Mr. Farrar preached from Isaiah xxxii., 2: 'A man shall be a hiding-place from the wind, and a covert from the tempest,'—with great effect. On the following Wednesday occurred a Quarterly Church Fast, which the church, it seems, had been accustomed to observe, not as the means especially of preparing the way for a revival, but for the general purpose of promoting their sanctification. This meeting* was attended by unwonted numbers, not only of the church but of others. Upon this assembly the Spirit came down in Pentecostal power. All were subdued. After the meeting was closed, the people did not disperse for nearly an hour, but stayed, anxious to converse on the subject of their own personal religion.† The report of what transpired at this meeting, as made by those who were present, had a thrilling effect upon the people generally. Such scenes were unknown in that day. None living had witnessed the like. Hence the novelty of the facts, as well as their intrinsic importance, deepened the interest of the occasion.

From this time through the winter, the work was 'with power.' The excitement was very great. The winter was severe and the snow deep, but it did not cool the burning zeal. Successive meetings were often held during the whole day, and by adjournment from one place to another. At these conference meetings, individuals would sometimes arise, and in their distress exclaim, · What *can* I do to be saved ?' So anxious were people to attend meetings that the sick were carried and laid on beds. Mr. Farrar attended these meetings as far as possible, and preached *without notes*—preached in tears, literally, and his auditors sobbing around him. In some cases, when private dwellings could not accommodate the many who attended, he would resort to the barn ; and with his auditors around him on the floor, and above him on the scaffold, dispense to them the word of life. So great was the demand for ministerial labor that clergymen from the neighboring churches came to the aid of the over-burdened pastor. The members of the church, also, were abundant in labors. They made it their

---

* At the house of Dea. Benjamin Adams, now Benjamin Clark's.

† When at length they left the house, those going north and west went together as far as the corner.—and there, winter evening though it was, stayed a long time in conversation before they could separate.

great business to converse with the impenitent to convert them to Christ. Young converts at once put on the harness as if enlisted in the *service* of Christ.

The time during which persons were under conviction in this revival is thought to have been about three weeks. The subjects of the work were of all ages, from children of four, seven and twelve years, up to extreme old age. And, if we may judge from such of them as have been living within the last twenty years, the conversions must have been genuine, and the consecration to Christ full and practical. So far as known, a solitary individual alone remains, a monument of the grace of this memorable period. As the fruits of this revival, there were added to the church during the year 1786, eighty-eight members, and in the year following, ten, by which the church was more than doubled, there being but ninety-one members before.

This work of grace was followed by revivals in neighboring places, especially in Temple,* Mason,† and Ashby. On election day, in 1786, the young people of New Ipswich went to Ashby to hold a religious meeting with the young people of that place. The minister of Ashby was present, as also Mr. Farrar, but the exercises were conducted chiefly by the young converts from New Ipswich. They told what God had done for their souls, and exhorted their young friends to repent.

There was no other revival during the ministry of Mr. Farrar, though it continued more than twenty years."

Others were added to the church in subsequent years,

---

* "The influence of the great revival in New Ipswich extended into Temple, and left precious and durable results."—[N.H. Churches, Temple.

† "About the year 1785, God in mercy visited this section of country and caused a great revival of religion in his people, and of his work in converting sinners, particularly in New Ipswich, under the ministry of the venerable Farrar. From this place the work extended to some other towns and churches; and this part of the vineyard was not wholly passed by, although it was in a deplorable state. Some few Christians in Mason were awakened, and began to apply themselves to their long-neglected duty; and many of the people, especially of the young, flocked to the solemn meetings in New Ipswich, and were filled with wonder. Soon some were convicted of sin, and became anxious for their souls' salvation, and after a time rejoiced in hope of pardoning mercy. But such was the state of the church in Mason, destitute of a minister, broken, dispirited, that the converts sought to unite with the church of New Ipswich, to which they had become tenderly attached by that acquaintance with the members which had been brought about by their intercourse, and by that mutual love which new-born souls, who have mourned and wept and prayed and rejoiced together, must feel. Their request was granted, on condition that they remove their relation whenever the church in Mason should become settled."—N. H. Churches, Mason.

some of whom unquestionably were converted in this revival. So that more than one hundred were gained to Christ
and his church by this blessed work of grace.

It may be stated as a fact not without interest, that the
winter was one of great severity. While hearts were
warm, the atmosphere was cold. The snow, also, was
very deep; the fences were covered; but the crust was
hard, and so strong that in passing from one religious
meeting to another in a different part of the town, for
instance, from a meeting at the house occupied by her
who was known to us as the Widow Abigail Davis, to a
meeting at the house of Silas Davis, on the Flat Moun-
tain, to be held an hour after the close of the first named,
the earnest people shortened their journey by a disregard
to roads. The hardened surface of the snow furnished a
good pathway for their feet.

The effects upon the future of a community of such a
transforming work must be very great. It transfers the
influence of many from the direction of death to that of
life. It gives a new character to many families. It
increases the number who attend public worship, and gives
intensity to the power of the pulpit. It creates a different
and favoring public sentiment, and thus indirectly shapes
the social and political character of a town. The causes
that originated in that revival have not only produced
their appropriate results here in the place of their birth,
but have gone forth in their sequences to do a great work
of good in shaping the character of communities in different parts of our country, and especially in the great West.

The piety of the converts in this revival must, of course,
partake largely of the characteristics of the piety of the
day. Much of the Puritan character remained in the
church, and was recognized by public sentiment as the ex-
emplification of the gospel. It was stern, and with a
strong tendency to gloom and doubts of personal accept-

ance—this last being judged of by the principles and processes of Edwards on the Affections. But it was the religion of principle. It thought more of duty, and less of privilege. It studied the law more than the promises. It partook more largely of godly fear than of the spirit of adoption. It was wanting, therefore, in that symmetry of religious character where the one is done and the other not left undone. I would not be understood to imply that there was not a good degree of unction in the piety of these our ancestors. The pastor was unlike *most* of the ministers of his day. His was a deeply experimental religion; and the utterances of his pulpit were eminently spiritual. By his lengthy ministry, and in so great a degree in the confidence of his church, he enstamped the impress of his own heart and spirit upon his flock. And they, like their pastor, were men of God. And some of them were the true children of Abraham, and believed the promises. A few of the subjects of this revival were, as has been said, among the living since the writer's connection with this church; and their gray hairs were "a crown of glory." One of them, a venerable mother in Israel,* converted at the age of twelve years in this revival, once told him her "experience," and that when light first broke in upon her mind from the Sun of Righteousness, it was so clear and unquestionable that she had no doubt that she loved the Saviour, "and," she added meekly, "I have never doubted it since." And they who have known her meek and humble life, and what was her influence upon her family—an influence that has passed down in blessings of almost unparalleled richness to the third and fourth generation—will not doubt the reality of the fact asserted.

And another fact related by her at the same interview

---

* Mrs. Stephen Brooks.

will illustrate somewhat the character, but especially the spirit, of that time. One Sabbath during the revival, the new-fallen snow was deep, and the path entirely unbroken. Could they go to meeting? (from the extreme southwest corner of the town.) Her father (Thaddeus Taylor) doubted. But she, in the ardor of childhood, was disposed to go; at any rate, the attempt could be made. So they started on horseback, she on a pillion behind her father. They got on as far as Mill Village, when from reports of the drifts beyond, the father was disposed to abandon the effort and return. Not so the daughter. " You get along with the horse, father, and I will get there myself," was her suggestion. And said she to me, " I got there—some of the way, indeed, on the fence, but I got there." The warm hearts and the physical state and habits of that day, may put to the blush the effeminacy of the young ladies now upon the stage.

And it may be added, in this connection, that the conversion of the Mr. Taylor, above named, introduced an era of religious prosperity to the neighborhood in which he lived, without the record of which the history of this church would be incomplete. This neighborhood includes the corners of three different towns, and is quite remote from the central place of worship in either. But in it was a school-house, and it was to them a house of God. In this house was often the preaching of the gospel by one of the pastors; also a Sabbath School in which the children, who had already been on foot five miles to meeting and to a Sabbath School, would again recite their Scripture lessons. And here, too, was occasionally the weekly prayer meeting; though oftener this was held in the several dwelling-houses. And this neighborhood, probably above any other in the town, was distinguished for its piety. In 1831, there were but two heads of families and scarcely any adults who were not professing Christians.

After this revival of 1785–6, nothing of special interest occurred during the ministry of Mr. Farrar. He kept on the even tenor of his way, and in the faithful discharge, according to the standard of that day, of the duties of his high calling. The duties of the sacred profession were less arduous then than now, and were chiefly confined to the two public services of the Sabbath, and pastoral visiting, of which much less was then expected than at the present day. There was also the Preparatory Lecture, and occasional meetings at the school-houses for catechising the children. But third meetings on the Sabbath, and weekly conference and prayer meetings, were not held. There was observed what was called the Quarterly Church Fast. This was on the First Wednesday of January, April, &c. In winter it was held in the evening; in summer, in the afternoon; and was, in its exercises, what are now Conference meetings. It was at one of these meetings, held, as has been said, at the house of Dea. Benjamin Adams, that was first developed into special external manifestation the deep feelings of the Great Revival. This Quarterly Church Fast was continued through the ministry of Mr. Farrar, and was observed at the time of the revival under the labors of Mr. Burbank and Mr. Hall. How long it continued, I do not learn.

It is a singular fact that, except the appointment of four Deacons, Mr. Farrar has made record of but one item of church business. June 28, 1804, the church voted an admonition to a delinquent member. If this was all the business of its kind the church had occasion to transact, how unlike its history under every succeeding pastorate!

Mr. Farrar died suddenly, of apoplexy, June 23d, 1809. At morning devotions, the fourth chapter of James was read. After the words, " Ye know not what shall be on the morrow. For what is your life? It is even a vapor,

D

that appeareth for a little time, and then vanisheth away," he paused, and looking around upon his family with an expression of unwonted interest, remarked upon the brevity and uncertainty of life, and upon the lessons which the fact should teach us. About 11 o'clock, A. M., as he came into his house,* and while standing in the northwest room, he said to his wife, " I feel as I never felt before," and instantly fell to the floor. He was for a short time insensible, but soon so far recovered as to be able to rise and stand ; when he remarked, " How good is ease after pain. This may be death, but if it is, there is nothing terrible in it." These were his last words. A second stroke rendered him insensible, and in about half an hour after the first attack, he ceased to breathe. He had often expressed the wish that he might die suddenly. The desire was realized.

The intelligence of his death shook the entire community like an earthquake. At first, all stood aghast. But after the first shock was past, reflecting men looked anxiously into the future. Said Judge Champney, referring to the state of the church, and to the pacific and controling influence of the venerable pastor—"Now there will be divisions." A Christian lady,† remembered by many now living as a mother in Israel, as she wiped away the fast-falling tears, said, "I am afraid there will be a division ; we shall never again be united, as we have been in Mr. Farrar." It was known that the elements for an effervescence were here, and might be in full operation now that the potent neutralizer was withdrawn. But we are anticipating. That future we shall soon meet face to face.

The relations of Mr. Farrar's ministry here as inceptive, and from its great length, extending through the formative

* Now occupied by C. C. Bellows.

† The Widow Abigail Davis, who died October 19, 1844, aged 90.

period of the town, render it proper that we devote special
attention to his character as a Christian pastor.

Rev. Stephen Farrar was a son of Dea. Samuel and
Lydia (Barrett) Farrar, of Lincoln, Mass. He was born
September 8, 1738. The house in which his father lived
is still standing, and owned by a descendant. He entered
Harvard College at the early age of thirteen, and conse-
quently graduated when but seventeen, in 1755. Theological seminaries were then unknown; but he pursued
the study of Theology, and at the age of eighteen began
to preach. In the winter of 1758-9, when but a few
weeks past twenty, he came to New Ipswich, and began
his work of more than fifty years. In the November following, as we have seen, he received his call; but was not
ordained till nearly a year afterward—October 22, 1760.
He married, November 29, 1764, Eunice Brown, daughter
of Isaac Brown, of Waltham, Mass., who survived him a
little more than nine years, and died September 9, 1818,
aged seventy-four. Their children were thirteen, one of
whom died in infancy. The others, eight sons and four
daughters, all lived to mature age, and were married.
From one of the two surviving daughters, a venerable
matron of fourscore and two years, we have learned many
of the facts incorporated into this history.

In person Mr. Farrar was in height about five feet eight
inches, neck short, head large, with high and intellectual
forehead, hair dark, eyes dark blue. In early life his
health was feeble, and his person slender. With years
his health improved, and he became large in proportion.
In the latter period of his life, he was broad spread and
even plethoric—still preserving, in a high degree, the symmetry of his form. It is supposed that at the time of his
death, he could not have weighed less than one hundred
and seventy-five or one hundred and eighty pounds. His
daughter thinks his health to have been so uniform that

he never, during his long ministry, lost a single Sabbath.

Intellectually, Mr. Farrar was much above mediocrity. This is the testimony of competent judges who heard him as a preacher. It is evinced in his manuscript sermons. That he entered college at thirteen years of age is evidence in point. That he could stand in the pulpit in New Ipswich, with men of such character for hearers, and retain their respect for half a century, shows that he had a superior intellect, as also common sense. These alone could have given him such influence and so long contiued—for it is among the modern innovations upon the theories of the fathers, that a minister should be dismissed because his talents and influence are so great. And finally, young men studied theology with him ; which shows that he had a reputation for superior professional attainments.

Socially, he was affectionate and kind. In his intercourse with society, he was dignified, and commanded the most profound respect, while yet he was affable, and, in the proper time and place, was facetious and even witty, but never light or frivolous. His appearance in the street commanded the reverence of all. As he walked along with his ivory-headed cane, dressed in his tri-cornered beaver, breeches, and white-topped boots, whoever met him made obeisance. But he was as courteous as he made others, always raising his beaver in respectful recognition, and especially to children and youth. When on the Sabbath he approached the meeting-house, all made way to the right and left for him, and uncovered their heads.

But while so venerable and awe-inspiring, he was, in his family, affectionate and winning. In the hours of relaxation, he played with his children, as if one of them. His daughter remembers when, with great glee, he would play " Run round the chimney " with her. But when he said, " That's enough," they were instantly hushed.

The social and sympathetic elements of his character were especially noticeable in his pastoral visitation. It was his rule to visit the families of his congregation once each year. In these visits he was freely communicative, giving utterance to his inmost heart. The remark made to the father of our venerable brother, John Binney, deceased, made with tears and sobs—" I have now been more than twenty years in my ministry here, and know not that I have done any good "—illustrates this habit of frankness. The natural correlate of such freedom, would be a similar habit in his people.

The piety of the venerable man was deep and pervading. The language just quoted illustrates this remark. It was the language of a heart full of sympathy with Christ, and of love for the souls of men. His sermons breathe the same spirit. And the tenderness and tears with which these sermons are said to have been delivered, could have no other significance. So of the fact that, at a day when revivals of religion were almost entirely unknown in the land, this congregation should receive so very rich a blessing as in 1786. It is evidence that the Word was preached with power, and from a warm and humble heart, that invited the presence and blessing of God. All that knew him, without any dissenting voice, so far as we know, speak of him as eminently a man of God. His piety began in early life, and grew with his growth; and would, in advanced life, exhibit peculiar richness and maturity.

As a preacher, Mr. Farrar excelled. His sermons were in the style of the day; and the divisions and sub-divisions and sub-sub-divisions were many. They were doctrinal and instructive, though practical and impressive. They were written, when for the pulpit. Occasional lectures were extempore. His manner in the pulpit was easy. Though earnest, he gestured but little, but was not con-lined to his notes. His voice was strong, but smooth and rich, and his organs of speech very much at command. He is said to have trilled the letter *r* with special grace. His preaching was the more impressive from the fact, so obvious, that his heart was in his utterances. Tears often accompanied his words; and all knew them to be the unaffected expression of the heart.

Mr. Farrar had much of the executive element. He accomplished much.

Though not a hard student, he was evidently familiar with the theological literature accessible at that day.

He wrote two sermons each week, and began the work of preparation for the Sabbath, Monday. He ordinarily devoted one day each to his sermons. He exchanged but little; once a year with the brethren in the neighborhood was the rule. He was settled with leave of absence two Sabbaths each year.

There is left to us his "account book," from his settlement to his death. From this we learn that he conducted the business of a farm, and had accounts with hired men and women, and also with his neighbors, in all the various articles produced by the husbandman. He also built and owned a grist-mill, and a malt-house, on the stream north of his house. After the opening of the Academy, in 1787, he took boarders. His daughter informs me, that at one time, the family that ate at his table consisted of thirty members. He was once the representative of the town at a Provincial Congress, and made three visits to Exeter in that capacity.

From the account book above alluded to, I infer that in the latter part of his life he had much less of secular business on his hands. There are almost no entries in the last ten years.

Such was the man, who, one hundred years ago this day,—this hour,—took upon himself the responsibilities of

Pastor of the Town of New Ipswich, and which he sustained during the long period of forty-eight years and
eight months. He was the minister of the town fifty
years and six months. Precious, venerable man! His
memory—it is the memory of the just—is blessed.

MR. HALL'S PASTORATE.

Immediately after the death of Mr. Farrar, the church
and the town entered upon the responsible, and to them
of that generation, new work of procuring a successor.
At a meeting of the church, July 29, 1809, of which Rev.
Seth Payson was moderator, it was " voted, to choose a
committee to join with a committee of the town, to procure a supply of preaching after the bearers have got
through in their course."

The reference in this vote is to a custom of that day,
that at the funeral of a pastor, the bearers should be neighboring pastors; and that these bearers should, each of
them, give to the bereaved church a Sabbath's service.

The first choice of the church and town was Rev. Experience Porter, who had been previously settled in Belchertown, Mass. The record is as follows:

" At a meeting of the church, July 19, 1810,
Chose the Rev. Seth Payson moderator.
Voted unanimously to give the Rev. Experience Porter a call to
settle with us in the work of a gospel minister.
Voted unanimously that the Selectmen be requested to call a meeting of the Town as soon as they may think proper, to see if the Town
will concur with the above vote, and will make suitable provision for
his support and maintenance."

The town voted to concur, and the call was in form extended to Mr. Porter.

But this so hopeful commencement had a less pleasing sequence. It is said that some unfavorable reports from abroad came to the ears of the good people. And moreover, Mr. Porter was not like Mr. Farrar—who, to many, was the standard of ministerial propriety. He was wanting in the serious and dignified gravity of Mr. Farrar, and especially were his white hose so unlike the black article they had been accustomed for more than fifty years to see ascend the pulpit stairs.

The disaffection continued to increase, till at length the town, which, in concurring with the church, had voted him a salary of five hundred dollars per annum and twenty-five cords of wood, met and rescinded the same, with but one dissenting vote. Soon after, (February, 1811,) he left town, having supplied the pulpit more than six months after his call. It is due to him to add, in this connection, that the public sentiment of the town afterwards awarded to him the reputation of injured innocence.

It was during Mr. Porter's labors here (1810) that the prayer meeting in the Davis neighborhood was commenced, which has continued with great regularity to the present day—*fifty years.* It might well celebrate its semi-centennial the present year.* May the generation to come carry it on to its centennial; and then, may it but have commenced: and on that hill-top may there be a weekly prayer meeting till the tabernacle of God shall be with men. Then, certainly, it will not cease.

A Mr. Burbank succeeded Mr. Porter as a supply for the pulpit. During his period of labor, commenced that so interesting revival into the midst of which it was the

---

* Since writing the above, a semi-centennial meeting has been held at the house of Joseph Davis, the place of the first meeting.

privilege of Mr. Hall, a few months after, to enter. Mr.
Burbank supposed himself a candidate, but was not so
regarded by the people. He was, in the first place, a man
of only ordinary talents. Besides, he entertained and
made very free and practical use of theological opinions,
that by no means harmonized with the doctrines that had
ever been inculcated in the New Ipswich pulpit. These
were brought into special prominence during the revival,
especially in the meetings for religious conversation held
at that time. There are persons now living who attended
these meetings, and remember well the things said. One
of the standing inquiries made by Mr. Burbank of those
who expressed hope was, "Are you willing to be damned?"
This was indeed a strait gate to the kingdom, a terrible
test of discipleship to Christ. In one case, the interrogated,
true to the instincts of his nature, uttered the necessary
truth, "*No.*" Mr. Burbank made his case the subject of
what he doubtless considered faithful remark, and held
him up to the meeting as deceived in his hope. In another
instance, a young lady answered the fearful question,
" Yes,"—mistaking, probably, at the moment, the feeling
of submission to God and willingness to suffer for his glory,
for the dreadful reality which her answer implied. She
went home, however, to reflect more at leisure upon the
subject, and became convinced that she was not " willing
to be damned." And she could not rest till she had informed her spiritual adviser that she had told him what
was not true, though the admission took from her her hope
in the Savior.

When Mr. Burbank left, and when Mr. Hall succeeded
in the supply of the pulpit, we cannot learn. Mr. Porter
supplied till February, when he left town. December 5th
succeeding, Mr. Hall received his call, and must have
preached some weeks previous—leaving only the spring

E

and summer months to Mr. Burbank. The following is the record of Mr. Hall's call:

" At a meeting of the church, Dec. 5th, 1811, The Rev. Cornelius Waters [of Ashby] was chosen Moderator.

Voted unanimously to give a Call to Mr. Richard Hall to settle with us in the work of a gospel minister, provided the Town can be honorably discharged from the Rev. Mr. Porter.

Voted unanimously that the Selectmen be requested to call a meeting of the Town, as soon as they think proper, to see if the Town will concur with the above vote, and will make suitable provision for his support and maintenance."

December 23d—The town voted to concur with the church in the call to Mr. Hall, and appointed a committee to correspond with Mr. Porter. That committee address him as follows:

" REV. AND DEAR SIR:—Since you left this place, we have been fortunate enough to find a candidate for the gospel ministry, in whom we are well united, and against whom no man has appeared to object. The gentleman we allude to, is Mr. Richard Hall. In consideration of this union of sentiment, the church held a meeting on the 5th inst., and voted unanimously to invite him to settle with us as pastor of this church and society, provided the Town could be honorably discharged from their obligations to you. On the 23d inst., the Town held a meeting, and voted to concur in the election of Mr. Hall, and directed us to send to you and procure such discharge. We have therefore, in the name and behalf of the Chh. and Town of N. Ipswich, to ask that you would have the goodness to send us, in answer, such a discharge as their feelings and wishes, under the circumstances, require, and as your benevolence will dictate.—We have only to add, that it is our constant wish and fervent prayer to God, that you may be soon happily established in some part of his vineyard, and that when you shall have filled a long life with usefulness, you may, through grace in Jesus Christ, be received to the rewards of the just."

Mr. Porter replies as follows:

" BELCHERTOWN, 7th Jany., 1812.
GENTLEMEN:—Your communication of the 26th ult. reached me this morning. I need not assure you that I rejoice to hear of your union

and prosperity in spiritual things. The prospect of my being settled
with you in the work of the evangelical ministry has long since van-
ished. An answer to the invitation which you communicated to me,
to this effect, from the chh. and society, would have been handed in
more than ten months past, but for the existence of extraordinary circumstances. These circumstances you cannot have forgotten ; it is
therefore needless to name them. If there be occasion to render an
apology for long delay, they furnish it.—The following was determined
on some time previous to my leaving N. Ipswich, in the month of
Feby., 1811 :

' Having taken into serious and prayerful consideration the invitation which I have received from the Chh. and Town of N. Ipswich to
settle with them in the work of the gospel ministry, I feel it a duty
which I owe to said Church and Town, and to myself and family, to
declare,—and I do hereby declare, that I cannot, under existing circumstances, accept of said invitation.'

This answer, gentlemen, ought no longer to be withheld from you.
You will make such use of it as occasion may require.

I would only add, that it is my constant wish and fervent prayer to
Almighty God, that the gentleman on whom you have fixed your
choice to be your pastor and teacher may prove a truly worthy successor of your late Revd. Pastor, and that both he and you, after many
years of distinguished usefulness and peace in the world, may be gathered to the congregation of the righteous in the kingdom of God.

Gentlemen, your servant in Christ Jesus,
EXPERIENCE PORTER."

This discharge obtained, the call to Mr. Hall was presented, and he replied as follows :

" To the Church and Town of New Ipswich :

Beloved Brethren and Friends :—By your committee I received an
invitation to settle with you in the gospel ministry. I have taken the
subject under serious consideration, have sought for divine direction,
and have consulted several of my fathers in the ministry. The result
is a thorough conviction of my duty. The harmony which has governed your proceedings and the conditions of the call are such as
induce me to declare a readiness to comply with your invitation.

Your liberality manifested for my support gives you a right to expect that I shall observe that exhortation of Paul to Timothy—' Give
attention to reading, to exhortation, to doctrine. Meditate upon these
things, give thyself wholly to them.' And now, commending you to

the grace of God, and requesting an unceasing remembrance in your prayers, that I may be faithful and successful in the arduous and infinitely momentous work to which I am called, I subscribe myself your affectionate friend and servant in the Lord,

RICHARD HALL.

N. Irswich, 25th Jany., 1812."

Mr. Hall was ordained March 12th, 1812. As a full and graphic account of this transaction is given in our Town History, it need not be repeated here. So of the new meeting-house, completed in the spring of 1813.

Mr. Hall entered upon his ministry in circumstances peculiarly favorable to success. The town constituted his charge—with the exception of a very few who were members of a Baptist church in Jaffrey. The town in its civil capacity were his supporters, and his salary was a part of its annual appropriation. The public mind was in a state pre-eminently favorable to impression from the labors of one educated in the improved methods of that day, and stored with the treasures to be acquired at—what was then new to New England—a Theological Seminary. That mind had not been seared by any of the methods of artificial excitement with which many congregations of a subsequent day were cursed. The ministry of his venerable predecessor had been one pre-eminently of inculcation. The people had been taught, rather than excited. And when now the young pastor, in the modified methods of his day and of the schools, addressed the motives of the gospel, they were the power of God to salvation. The truth fell like good seed into good ground, and brought forth an hundred-fold. It had been now nearly thirty years since there had been a revival. A generation had grown up, indoctrinated, but not impressed. Such a community would be moved by a revival and the breath of the Spirit, as the heavy ripened harvest of the field bends before the wind.

As we have said, a revival was already in progress when
Mr. Hall began his labors as a candidate. The Spirit was
here. Not a few were indulging hope. All the tenderness of such a state belonged to the public mind. All
this was pre-eminently favorable to the young candidate.
Himself would feel the inspiration, and preach as he could
not in ordinary circumstances. And then the preaching,
—even if it had been but ordinary,—was addressed to
accepting ears and loving hearts. No wonder the union
of the parties was firm. No wonder the love of each was
strong in life and strong in death.

As the fruit of the revival, there were added to the
church within one year from the ordination of Mr. Hall,
about one hundred persons.

Again in 1821–2 was another revival of great power ;
and about fifty were soon after added to the church.

It was during the labors of this revival that Mr. Hall's
health began to fail, and in May following, while preaching the sermon before an ordaining council in Bradford,
N. H., he was seized with hemorrhage of the lungs. He
preached no more. As a means of improving his health,
he spent a winter at the South, and in the following summer came the whole way from New Orleans to New Ipswich on horseback. But the disease was past cure.

The closing period of his connection with the church
and town was one of sadness and grief on his part. The
history of this period is faithfully given in the history of
our town.

The following obituary notice of Mr. Hall, from the pen
of Dr. Lord, President of Dartmouth College, but then of
Amherst, will give a better idea of the personal character
of this good man and faithful pastor than any thing that
could be said by one that knew him less intimately :

" DIED—At New Haven, Vt., in July last, (13th, 1824,) while on
a visit to his friends, Rev. Richard Hall, of New Ipswich, N. H., and

Pastor of the Congregational Church in that place. Mr. Hall had languished about two years under a severe pulmonary complaint, induced by excessive labors during a period of unusual religious excitement among his people, in the winter and spring of 1822. A robust frame was suddenly struck at the vital part. While addressing an ordaining council at Bradford, N. H., in May of that year, he was seized with hemorrhage at the lungs, which terminated his active services as a minister, and gradually wore out his life. Mr. Hall was a native of Mansfield, Conn., 1784. His parents afterwards removed to Vermont, where he received his early education. He was graduated at Middlebury College in 1808, having sustained the character of a diligent, exemplary and highly respectable scholar. The office of Tutor was immediately given him, in which, after spending one year, and nearly three years in preparatory studies for the ministry at the Theological Institution at Andover, he was ordained at New Ipswich in March, 1812. The piety of Mr. Hall was unquestionable. At the age of twelve years, he received those religious impressions which resulted, as he hoped, in his conversion to God, a change which is said to have been strongly and decisively marked. He was united to the church at sixteen, and both in his life and death he witnessed a good confession.

To recollect traits of character which have made any conspicuous in their profession and useful to mankind, and which, through the influence of Christian principle, as in the present instance, have served to adorn the Gospel, is always due to the cause of religion and humanity.

Possessed of a superior intellect, and governed by a high sense of moral obligation, Mr. Hall gave himself with singleness and assiduity to his ministry. He cultivated his mind, and made it bear upon every department of his office. He brought to his public performances the matter of theology with great accuracy of language, precision of statement, power of argument, pertinence, force, and honesty of application. In ecclesiastical affairs, he was an able counsellor and a firm executor. He had influence among his brethren and the churches of Christ. His opinions contributed to give weight to their deliberations, and effect to their decisions. The church under his care was almost constantly receiving accessions, and was among the foremost in pious and benevolent exertions. Integrity and decision were prominent features of his character. His mind, just in its discriminations, and patient in its inquiries, was accustomed to fix presently upon the few simple and naked principles of truth; and by these his habits were regulated. Having satisfied himself about the right and the wrong, he was then never affected by circumstances, in the performance of duty. He went

in the straight-forward path, neither asking nor showing favor. Too
fond of the right to pursue the expedient, he hesitated not while other
men were consulting the maxims of worldly prudence. He cared for
what he viewed as truth or duty ; he cared not for the consequences
of maintaining the one or performing the other. Rigor in such char-
acters may occasionally be excessive. But it is a failing that ' leans
to virtue's side,' and proves the existence of those qualities without
which men are always unprincipled and injurious. Mr. Hall's hardi-
hood of character did not, however, grow out of pride or obstinacy.
He followed not the impulse of a blind self-will. Of course, he was
consistent. He was always the same in the various relations of life.
It was known where he might be found, and that confidence in him
would not be misplaced. His mind was not the most accessible, but
being understood, it was trusted. It was not expected that he would
renounce his principles or counteract them.

He knew that power is in reason and truth, whose action, though
slow and interrupted, through the various errors and prejudices of
men, will issue in the general welfare of society, and the recovery of a
lost world to Him who bought it with his blood. It was natural that
a mind thus intent upon high objects and great results should be
hardly disturbed by the changes of life, or by those matters of light
and uncertain import, which so much engage the attention and affect
the dispositions and conduct of the generality of men. Such qualities,
by all who rightly estimate human character, will be thought more
valuable than those external accomplishments to which many men
have owed a greater celebrity. Mr. Hall's worth was not all apparent.
Others have had more refinement, and have displayed better before the
world, but few have had his solidity and strength. His place in
society, in the church of God, was among the supports, not the decora-
tions. The loss of such men usually continues to be felt. To the community it is great ; to their families it is irreparable."

It was in Mr. Hall's ministry that a change took place
in the mode of admission to the church, as also in the
creed of the church. In accordance with the practice of
the Pilgrim Fathers, and early churches of New England,
during Mr. Farrar's ministry, the creed was a thing of
church record, by a reference to which the doctrinal basis
of the church could be learned. And when persons applied for admission to the church, the first question, and

the chief, related to their personal character. And since they applied for admission to the church, they did avow an assent to the doctrines taught from its pulpit, so far, that they could be edified by the preaching, and enjoy themselves in the fellowship of those who were of this faith. They assented to the creed " for substance of doctrine," as the phrase was. More than this was not required. And they were admitted to the church merely by a public acceptance of, and assent to, the covenant.

At a meeting of the church held July 1, 1819, a committee was chosen " to prepare for the consideration of the church a Confession of Faith." This committee reported to the church, November 4th, what are now the Confession of Faith and Covenant of the Church. The Confession was read and considered article by article; and without coming to a vote, the church adjourned till the 16th of that month. At this meeting it was twice read and discussed at length; and finally adopted unanimously. The Covenant was then considered, and adopted unanimously.

" Then voted, that our Confession of Faith and Covenant be publicly assented to by every one who shall hereafter unite with this church, not having previously made a public profession of religion. Also, voted,

That no member of any other church shall become a member of this without consenting to our Confession of Faith by subscribing it."

I find in the files of the church a printed Confession and Covenant, upon which is written the following: "It is a standing rule in the church, that members received from other churches, subscribe to our Confession of Faith." To this is attached several blank leaves containing names of persons admitted by letter, from May 4th, 1820, to March, 1833. This list embraces but a part of the persons received by letter during this period. But the presumption is, that the practice, which, it seems, during its continuance, was but imperfect, fell into disuse about 1833. The present pastor has known nothing of it.

The elder portion of my audience will remember that this measure of introducing a creed into the form of admission to the church was at a time when the more evangelical portion of the New England churches had just become thoroughly aware of, and excited by the fact of a great declension from what they regarded sound orthodoxy, and were astir in the effort to eliminate from the faith of their fathers this admixture of error. Creeds of rigid angular precision were brought into great prominence. Our creed, as we all know, is one of metaphysical exactness.

That such creeds, and so used, may have been of service in the circumstances in which ours originated, we will not deny. But that in ordinary circumstances such a creed, to be publicly assented to by all—even little children—as part of the formula of admission to the church, is proper, we do not believe. Neither the Bible nor a sound philosophy, nor good common sense sanction it. Such a creed, as on the record of the church, is right. That is its place. But we go for the practice of the Puritans—the practice of our fathers of this church for the first sixty years of its existence. The solemn sacred covenant of Mr. Farrar's day has our decided preference. Would that this church might accept it. They could not do a better thing now in the beginning of this new century, than to re-adopt this "form of sound words" by which their fathers and mothers vowed to be the Lord's before heaven and earth.

With Mr. Hall's ministry terminated the support of the institutions of religion by the town. The "Congregational Church and Society" was organized in 1824, and has taken the place of the town in the support of the ministry in concurrence with the church.

In Mr. Hall's day began the Sabbath School. This, like

so many religious institutions of the present day, had its origin in a feeble germ, and involved but a part of the influence for good that attends upon its operations at the present day, with its Question Books, Commentaries, Libraries, and its literature of every kind, and with its monthly concert of prayer.

The Sabbath School in this place owed its origin to the Christian zeal of the sisterhood. In the summer of 1818, the good mothers gave it birth, and secured the appointment of Dea. Clark as superintendent. But in the succeeding winter it was suspended. Like Nature, in some of her functions, it was "frozen up." When, however, spring returned, the interest of the brethren was not re-vivified; and the good women had again the honor of the initiative. After talking themselves into a mood sufficiently executive, they, one Sabbath noon, gathered each as many children as possible, and went into the Town Hall. They organized by the appointment of the Widow Abigail Davis, superintendent, then made arrangements for future operation, and adjourned. But all this could not be done and escape observation. Said one of the brethren to a sister still living, as they were returning home after the close of service, "Was n't there a meeting at the Town Hall this noon-time?" Her answer embraced the history just given. As well he might, he lifted both hands and exclaimed, "Why, you shame us almost to death!" The sluggishness of the brethren was now overcome, and they at once proceeded to organize again a regular Sabbath School, and Dea. Clark was again made the superintendent. It has never since been "frozen up" in winter, but continued without interruption to the present day.

MR. BARBOUR'S PASTORATE.

Mr. Hall was succeeded by Rev. Isaac R. Barbour, whose call, settlement and dismission all belong to the melancholy portion of our history.

October 4th, 1824, the church "give Rev. Isaac R. Barbour a call to settle with us in the work of the gospel ministry," and request the "Society to concur therein, and to stipulate the terms of support." The Society did not concur, and the call therefore was incomplete. Mr. Barbour, however, continued to labor on as a supply for more than a year, and on the 28th of November, 1825, the church renewed the call by a vote of "24 in favor, 9 or 10 neuter." On the 14th of December, and previous to any action of the society, another meeting of the church was held, and the call renewed by a vote of "35 in favor, 5 neuter." In this the society concurred, and on the Sabbath next preceding January 9, 1826, Mr. Barbour negatived the call. February 4th, the society voted to "choose a committee to unite with a committee that may be chosen in the church, to request the Rev. Isaac R. Barbour to withdraw his answer which negatived their call, and accept the same as heretofore given." The church concurred by a vote of "19 in favor, 8 against, 3 neuter." This call was accepted, February 12, and the Installation took place March 8. Objections to the installation were made to the Council by the opposers, and the Council were not unanimous in their vote to proceed.

The future of a relation instituted in such a method were easily foretold. The persistent minority were persistent still. And in the various methods at the command of minorities, attempted to effect the dissolution of the connection which they had tried so earnestly to prevent. And it was only August 22d—less than six months after his installation—that the pastor asked a dismission, and the church at the same meeting voted their acceptance, and appointed a committee to carry the same into effect, which was done in the following month. The church made to Mr. Barbour at the time of his dismission a present of $150 ; also purchased his real estate.*

Mr. Barbour was a native of Bridport, Vt., and educated at Middlebury College. After his dismission from this church, he was installed pastor of the church in Byfield, Mass., December 20, 1827, and subsequently was a city missionary in Boston.

MR. WALKER'S PASTORATE.

The fourth Pastor of this church was Rev. Charles Walker, a young graduate direct from the Theological Seminary at Andover. His commencement here was more auspicious than that of his predecessor. His first impressions were favorable, and his call very unanimous and cordial. It was dated December 20, 1826. The salary offered by the society was six hundred dollars. To this sum the church, as such, added one hundred dollars. He was ordained February 28, 1827. The Council was composed of the representatives of the churches in Temple, Jaffrey, Mason, Hollis, Theological Seminary of Andover, Mass., Townsend, Mass., Lyndeborough, Amherst, Alstead, Keene, Rindge, Ashby, Mass., and the former pastor of this church, Rev. I. R. Barbour. Rev. Eli Smith, of Hol-

---

* The house now occupied by Richard Wheeler.

lis, was Moderator of Council, and Rev. Z. S. Barstow, of Keene, Scribe. Dr. Woods, of Andover, preached the sermon.

The following extract from the minutes of Council may be of interest as an item of the history of the times:

" The Council unanimously passed the following resolution : Whereas, it is of great importance that ministers of the gospel and private Christians should do all in their power to discountenance the customary use of intoxicating liquors, the evils of which are spreading such desolation through our country, and greatly injuring the cause of religion, therefore Resolved, that this Ecclesiastical Council request the Committee of this Church and Society to exclude all ardent spirits and wines from the provisions that shall be made for the entertainment of this Council."

Among the first acts of Mr. Walker's ministry was the effort to enlist a greater amount of lay agency in the work of the Lord, and in co-operation with the pastor. April 10, 1827, it was " Voted to have the deacons associated with the pastor in particular attendance to those who are entertaining hopes "—a measure judicious and expedient only on the hypothesis that the deacons are men distinguished at once by superior intelligence and piety. There is no more delicate work for the experienced pastor than that of conversing with the plastic minds of persons in the great crisis. Advice such as that said to be given by Mr. Burbank to the babes in Christ, would probably reduce them to invalidship, and dwarf them for life. And given before conversion, it might—its tendency would be to drive them into rebellion and a hopeless distance from God and heaven.

June 21, 1827, it was " voted to choose a committee to visit the members of the church and others to converse particularly on the subject of religion." This committee consisted of two in each school district ; and after their designation and appointment, it was voted "to hold a church conference in three weeks from this date, in order that we may more fully know the state of religion among us."

October 4, 1827, "Voted that a *Committee of Examination* be appointed. It shall consist of five, and be appointed by a nominating committee. Their duty shall be to make inquiry whether there are any thoughtful, anxious or hoping; to converse with them and with the pastor and one another in relation to them ; to meet at inquiry meetings, and in examining candidates for being propounded."

At the same meeting, it was "voted to choose a committee to attend to public offences." This committee was to consist of four, and "be in office one year." Their duty is to "attend to all cases of public offence, i. e. such offences as are generally known, and in relation to which many are aggrieved. They will converse together and with the pastor in regard to particular cases, and endeavor to devise and execute the most scriptural method of commencing and conducting discipline." This committee received new appointments in 1829, 1830, 1831, and in 1832 were made permanent till others were chosen.

Four years afterwards, "March 3, 1831, it was voted that the Committee of Examination meet statedly about four weeks previous to the communions."

These two committees are the same as those now known as the Committee of Examination and the Committee of Discipline, and have continued from that day to this.

These arrangements had their origin, in part doubtless, in correct principles of the importance of lay agency in the church, and in the desire to develop that power for the salvation of the world, so great in the normal state of the church, but so much of which is yet latent. But I cannot doubt that a constitutional timidity in the pastor, that shrank from responsibility, had much to do with this division of it between himself and others.

Mr. Walker's pastorate embraced one of the most interesting periods, and one most favorable to the ends of the Christian ministry—the period of revivals and of protracted meetings. And as his predecessors had been men distinguished for sound orthodoxy, deep piety, and professional fidelity, the seed had been sown in New Ipswich, that, under the Christian culture of so good a man, must spring up and bear a precious harvest. Protracted meetings were held repeatedly, and conversions were numerous. Large additions were made to the church in the years 1831 and 1832. In 1834, Rev. Mr. Foote, the then celebrated revivalist, was invited to conduct a protracted meeting. He could not come at the time proposed. A few weeks later, the question of inviting him again to hold a protracted meeting in this place was brought before the church and a vote taken, of which the following is the record : " This vote was put twice, and both brethren and sisters voted, and it stood the last time as follows : six in favor and ten neutrals. Also voted, That the Pastor inform Rev. Mr. Foote how the vote stands." This was October 9, 1834. We are happy to find evidence of an estimate of men and things so just as that evinced in this vote..

But there were sad drawbacks upon the pleasantness of Mr. Walker's ministry. The first meeting of the church after the ordination was on the business furnished by a case of discipline. And during his ministry of eight years, there were one hundred and six church meetings on business ; many of them, I am told, continued till late at night, and most of them occupied with the same painful work. A discipline mania seemed to prevail in the church. There were few cases of any serious importance, or that compromised Christian character. Trifles, that merited only to be put to the account of human imperfection and to be forgotten, were magnified and brought with solemn, pompous formality before the church ; and after wrangling examination and discussion, referred to councils. The famous case of "Brother Josiah Reed" had its commencement August 13, 1829, and continued to disturb the peace and irritate the temper of the church for more than five years. It received a final disposition not till after the dismission of Mr. Walker. Complaints the most vague and indefinite were brought, and the church had the weakness to entertain them ; and in the conduct of them, allowed itself to be outraged by the grossest indecorum of some of the members. The pastor, with all the rich assemblage of excellences that composed his character, and that so justly won the ardent love of the good people of his charge, was yet wanting in those qualities that constitute a good moderator of a large church in turbulent times. He wanted firmness and courage. And in cases when it belonged to the gubernatorial function to decide and dispose of and proceed, his language was, "Brethren, what shall we do?" And the brethren were, as a matter of course, like their leader ; and all was indecision and confusion.

Effervescence was a necessary consequence of such a state of things. Wrangling and contention ensued. Brother disciplined brother; and finally the pastor was made a participator in this fashionable treatment. He was dragged before the church, and in a manner at once insulting to both the church and pastor,—and for the veriest nothing. And had the church acted on the principle of attending to cases really deserving notice and rejecting others—instead of the opposite policy—the agitator in this case would have been put to silence in brief order. But the case went up to a council, and from that received a rebuke in the direction where it was deserved. And the meek and Christian spirit of the pastor was recognized and commended.

Factions grow of course in such a soil and with such a

culture. It was so here. And although the great body
of the church loved their pastor, there were those whose
object it was to destroy his peace and hinder his usefulness. And while he ought, had he been a different man,
to have stood and calmly performed his work, relying on
the promise, "Lo, I am with you always," yet being what
he was, he could not. What is one man's duty in given
circumstances, is not always the duty of another in the
same. Mr. Walker could not stand and labor in the pelt-
ing storm. The first dash was fatal. He fled ; and as he
fled, he went prone, and not to rise, and soon was pros-
trate. The mortal wound had been inflicted. He died a
victim.

Mr. Walker first publicly announced his wish to be dismissed, Sabbath, June 14, 1835, as follows :

" A question of no common interest has agitated my mind for a
considerable time past. It is whether 1 shall seek a dissolution of the
connexion which binds me to my beloved people. I have endeavored
to seek divine direction—me t the question fairly and examine it in its
various aspects. I have looked at general principles—sought for facts
—noticed the spirit of the age and the elements at work in the public
mind ; and have settled in the following general principles :

1. Ministers are the property of the church at large.

2. Whenever serious obstacles exist to their usefulness in any place,
they are at liberty to seek a dismission ; whatever be the nature of
those obstacles.

3. A stranger may sometimes preserve harmony and prevent sehisms
in a church, which the Pastor for the time being may attempt in vain.

In applying these general principles to my own case, I find

1. That there are obstacles to my highest degree of usefulness. Of
the nature of these obstacles I have nothing to say.

2. If I should leave this place, and the great Master of the vineyard
has any thing for me to do, his Providence will doubtless point me
to the spot.

3. Should you unite in another man, as I ardently hope you may,
he will be likely to labor to greater advantage than your present
Pastor can.

G

In view of these things I am induced to call a church meeting on Thursday next at 4 o'clock, for the purpose of choosing a Council to dissolve the connexion between us as pastor and people.

I make this communication in this public manner, that all may distinctly understand the grounds on which I desire a dismission. It is not to escape from trials—or because I have another place in view,—or because my friends are not ready to sustain me. But simply, so far as I know myself, with the ardent hope that it may be for the good of the people.

Perhaps I have mistaken the path of duty—if so, I stand ready to be corrected. But unless something different, and of a marked character appear, I cannot change my ground : and unless there be special occasion for it, I earnestly request my friends to acquiesce in my decision, to say nothing to me on this painful subject : and however unexpected it may be to others, it is no hasty course with the Pastor."

At the church meeting the succeeding Thursday, he presented the following :

" TO THE CONGREGATIONAL CHURCH IN NEW IPSWICH :

MY DEAR BRETHREN :—You are already apprised of my design in calling the present meeting. It is to request a dissolution of the relation I hold to you as Pastor. I know, and I deeply feel that this is a sacred and an endearing relation ; and it is with long and anxious reflection and inquiry that I have taken this step. Be assured it is not because my confidence or interest in you have diminished, or my affection abated. Far otherwise. Should you see fit to comply with my request, I should then be ready to join with you in calling a Council to dissolve the connection.

Your affectionate Pastor,
C. WALKER."

The motion was made " *Not* to comply with the Pastor's request." Before voting on the question, the meeting was adjourned for one week. At this meeting the motion of the previous week was passed in the affirmative. In the language of the record : " Of the 61 brethren present, 55 voted in the affirmative. The others did not vote at all. As it was desired that the sisters should manifest their

minds, 61 arose in the affirmative. A few did not arise."
A committee was appointed to report the doings of the
meeting to the pastor. This committee say :

" Against granting your request was urged the difficulty of obtain-
ing a stranger as pastor, who would more firmly unite the church and
society for any length of time, and contribute more to the good of the
whole, than had been done in years past. The frequent exchange of
ministers, so common at the present day, was thought to be a great
evil, one that encourages a spirit of dissatisfaction and disunion on
very slight grounds ; that injures the usefulness of many ministers,
and undermines the foundations of society. The church, in general,
appeared to feel perfectly satisfied with their present Pastor, and voted
by a large majority, against complying with his request.
ISAAC ADAMS,
E. H. FARRAR,
CHARLES SHEDD."

This letter had only the effect of suspending for a brief
period the process. On the 19th July, the pastor from the
pulpit renewed his request, as follows :

" To the Congregational Church and Society in New Ipswich :
Dear Friends :—Some weeks since, in calling a church meeting, I
stated to the congregation that I should ask a dismission : and the
grounds on which I should make the request.
When the church acted upon this request, it was in a very united
manner not to grant it. This vote led me to pause, that I might learn
what Providence meant by it. Perhaps I am slow to learn, or look
through false mediums, but I can, as yet, discover no sufficient reason
why I should change the ground which I took at first. Although the
obstacles to my usefulness are not so great as I apprehended, still there
are obstacles to my highest degree of usefulness. The confidence and
affection which you have shown, greatly endear you to me, and had I
yielded to the impulse of my own feelings, I should have withdrawn
my request at once. But there are a great many things to be taken
into the account in settling a matter of this kind. I have endeavored
carefully to review the ground I have taken, and am satisfied in my
own mind, that it will be best, all things considered, that our connexion as Pastor and people should be dissolved. I would therefore

appoint a church meeting on Thursday next at 2 o'clock, for the purpose of acting upon a renewed request.

Your affectionate Pastor,

C. WALKER."

At this meeting of the church, the request was again made in form for a dismission. It was referred to a committee, who presented the following resolutions :

" Resolved 1. That our Pastor retains our entire confidence, in respect to his talents, his ministerial, social and Christian character.

2. That we deeply regret that any causes should exist which render it expedient in his view to take up his connection as Pastor with us. Considering, however, that it is his earnest and repeated request, we yield our consent, though with much reluctance."

The record adds, " The first resolution, without hesitation, passed in the affirmative ; the second was negatived. But after a long discussion, the negative vote was recalled, and this also passed in the affirmative."

The following is an extract from the doings of the Council that dismissed :

" While the Council, in view of existing circumstances, deeply regret the necessity of coming to this result, they desire to express the high sense they entertain of the piety, talents and ministerial qualifications of Rev. Mr. Walker, and hereby most cordially recommend him to the church of Christ, wherever God in his providence shall call him, as an *able*, *faithful*, *devoted* and *successful* minister of the Lord Jesus."

Thus ended the connection of a pastor with a church and people the greatest part of whom loved him tenderly, a pastor who—in their own words—" retained their entire confidence in respect to his talents, his ministerial, social and Christian character,"—and with whom they are " perfectly satisfied,"—a pastor whom God had greatly owned and blessed, so that under his ministry the church had been borne upward to a position of prosperity never before attained.

Why then was he dismissed? We think it is to be ascribed to an erroneous theory of this good man,—a theory prevalent at that day, and that has brought disaster upon very many of the churches of our land,—that, as a pastor's " highest degree of usefulness " depends upon the unanimous confidence of his people, he must therefore be dismissed if even a very few are, for any reason, good or bad, dissatisfied. It might as well be said that a pastor's " highest degree of usefulness " depended upon a willingness in his hearers, without an exception, to accept the conditions of salvation on first presentation from his lips ; and that if all did not thus accept and become the genuine disciples of the Savior, the minister should be dismissed, and seek some field of labor where this beatific theory of " the highest degree of usefulness " could be realized. It is understood that Mr. Walker's theory on this subject experienced subsequently a great change, and was in conformity with what has since been the theory and the practice of the church he left.

And it may be remarked, as an explanation in part of the ceaseless agitations of the church during Mr. Walker's ministry, that he failed entirely to recognize the independence and final and decisive authority of Congregational churches. The church and its pastor seemed ever to consider themselves as amenable to the *authoritative* supervision of Councils. Certainly his successor in the pastorship found this the theory of the church. Hence any unprincipled and ambitious disturber of the peace of the church could keep them in perpetual apprehension of Councils, and prevent any decisive and final action that could put a matter to rest. Such disturbers and such disturbance the church had. And there were, during the years of Mr. Walker's ministry, in addition to the one hundred and six church meetings for business, two mutual Councils, one *ex parte* Council, and two ecclesiastical References—five in all. These, of course, do not include the ordaining and dismissing Councils.

Rev. Charles Walker was born in Rindge, N. H., Nov. 21, 1795. He was the son of a farmer of moderate means, and who, while this son was yet in his childhood, lost his property, and was reduced to poverty. Charles, the youngest of a large family, was left to shirk for himself. He earned his living by the labor of his hands. The "two or three last years of his minority" he spent in New Ipswich, in the service of Everett & King, woolen manufacturers. At the age of twenty-one years and six months, (in the spring of 1817,) he began to prepare for College at Kimball Union Academy. He graduated at Dartmouth in 1823, and at Andover Seminary in 1826, and came directly from that Seminary to this place.

His parents were not professors of religion, but regular attendants upon public worship. The only professedly religious member of the family was an elder sister, whose influence on his heart was very great. He remarked near the close of life, that he then remembered the religious truth he learned from this faithful sister.

He seems, when yet quite young, to have had a deep interest in the subject of religion, and to have read and re-read such authors as Edwards, Newton and Boston—old books that were in his father's library. At this early period the scenery of his native place had a strong religious influence upon him. He saw God in it. He joined Dr. Payson's church when fifteen years of age, but could not tell when he was converted. He had no "experience" to relate ; but he loved the Bible and the God of the Bible, and Nature and the God of Nature.

Mr. Walker was a man of fair talents, a good writer, and a faithful and impressive preacher. He was, for the best of reasons, greatly beloved by many in New Ipswich. And in return he gave his heart's love to this people. On this point he said a short time before his death, "My fields of labor were all of them pleasant, but more especially New Ipswich. It was a season of great trial and hard labor, it is true, but of great blessings."

After his dismission from this church, he was settled, March 9, 1836, at Windsor, Conn.; again, in 1837, in Medfield, Mass., and dismissed in 1838; again, in Wells, Me., and dismissed May 16, 1844. The winter of 1845 he spent in Italy, being absent about five months. After this he cultivated a farm in Groton, Mass., where he died October 23, 1847. These, so many installations and dismissions in such rapid succession, illustrate the nature and tendency of the principles on which he acted in seeking a dissolution of his connection with the church of his first love.

The following minute is appended by Mr. Walker to the list of members in the Church Records: "In 1827, number of members 173. From my settlement, Feb., 1827, to Feb., 1835, 8 years, there were 173 added by profession; 131 of whom were baptized in their infancy; 43 by letter. About 50 removals and deaths." "June, 1834, 306,"—i. e., I suppose, the number of the church was three hundred and six.

MR. LEE'S PASTORATE.

The following is an extract from the record of the church, January 18, 1836 :

" A subject was presented by the moderator for consultation, as to the *propriety* or *expediency* of calling a man to settle with us as a minister of the gospel, without attending to the usual preliminary course of probation. After some little consultation, it was moved and seconded that we present Rev. Samuel Lee, of Sherburne, Mass., a call to settle with us in the work of the gospel ministry.

The above motion was carried into effect by vote of the church."

This call was to him who received it one of many similar applications claiming his attention about that time. He was the pastor of a beloved and confiding church, and with an adequate support. Why he accepted this call has ever been to him a profound mystery. He is a believer in a very special and controlling power of the Spirit of the Lord, and thinks that the Lord had a work to be done in New Ipswich for which he was especially fitted ; and that the mighty Spirit, almost against his will, dictated an affirmative answer to the call. And he came. And now the last sands of the last year of a quarter of a century are fast running. So far as he is or ever has been able to analyze his own heart at the time, the one weight—placed by the Spirit of God in the scale—that was decisive, was the fact that this was a wide field that would put in requisition a large amount of toil. To toil was then the ruling passion of the mind that now longs for rest.

The installation took place on the 5th of May. The Council was composed of delegates from the churches in Mason, Hollis, Wilton, Temple, Rindge, Keene ; and in

Massachusetts, from Ashburnham, Ashby, Pepperell and Sherburne. The Council met at five o'clock in the afternoon of Wednesday, the 4th, and the examination of the candidate was in the evening. The public services were Thursday, at eleven o'clock.

The following is the creed presented to the Council by the candidate at his examination:

"I believe in one God, Father, Son and Holy Ghost—three persons in one God.

I believe that the book, which we call the Bible, is a revelation from God.

I believe that God is administering a moral government over man under an economy of grace, through an Atonement; and that this Atonement was made by the death of the Lord Jesus Christ.

I believe that the purposes of God extend to all events.

I believe that God has, from eternity, elected a part of mankind to salvation through sanctification of the Spirit, and belief of the truth.

I believe that all men are entirely destitute of holiness until regeneration; and that regeneration is secured by the special and direct influences of the Holy Spirit.

I believe that all who are thus regenerated, will so persevere unto the end, as finally to be saved.

I believe in a future state of endless rewards and punishments.

I believe that Baptism and the Lord's Supper are Sacraments of the New Testament,—that baptism is to be administered to adult believers and their infant children—and that the Sacrament of the Lord's Supper is to be administered only to believers who have made a credible profession of their faith in Christ."

The new pastor found himself in a condition of intense interest; some of the circumstances of which were quite peculiar.

Unlike those whose call was preceded by a period of candidateship, he had yet to make upon those whose pastor he now was, an impression of himself as a preacher. Would he suit their taste, and win their love? or awaken their aversion?

And then the past and the present, as well as this un-

H

certain future. The past had been blessed and was hallowed in review. He had come from the warm bosom of a beloved and loving church. Pastor and church had given, each to the other, the warmth and the tenderness of first love, and their life and labors together had been those of rare success. In leaving them the dismissed pastor had "dragged a lengthening chain."

But now he was a stranger in a strange land. Could he love as he had loved, or be loved as he had been loved? What experience has proved possible and made actual, then seemed impossible. And he felt himself alone and unsupported save by the Almighty Arm. But he was ardent and determined. And he loved above, infinitely above all other employments, to preach the gospel and perform the duties of a christian pastor. And that the field was wide, and that it was of difficult culture, were rather incentives than discouragements. And after he had, like the homesick child, wept till his heart was relieved, he girded up the closer his armor, and addressed himself to his work, and felt "strong in the Lord and in the power of his might." He went out upon the solemn future, not doubting that the God of Abraham had led him to this as the promised land, and would be with him while he made it the field of his culture. And—it should be recorded—it has been so.

Several changes in the administration of the church occurred in the early part of his ministry.

March 2, 1837, a committee to whom had been referred the question of exchanging "Watts' and Select" for "Church Psalmody" in the worship of the sanctuary, reported in favor of the change, and it was adopted. In July following was commenced the practice of observing Quarterly Church Meetings "for religious conference, and at which, if necessary, any business of the church might be transacted."

At this first Quarterly Meeting was adopted unanimously the following : " That candidates for admission to the church be examined by the Committee of Examination, and if by them approved, be propounded three weeks at least previous to the time of admission ; and if during this time there be no objections made, that they be admitted without further formality."

From the first it had been the practice of the church, that candidates for membership should appear before the church itself for examination. At their option, they related their experience verbally or in writing; and might then be questioned by any of the members.

We have seen that in 1827 a Committee of Examination was chosen, and that in 1831 it was made the duty of this committee to " meet statedly about four weeks previous to the communions." The labors of this committee were at first informal. But after 1831 candidates for admission were expected to meet them for examination ; then again to meet the church for the same purpose. By the method now adopted this last was dispensed with, and in its stead the candidate was propounded from the pulpit, and silence assumed as consent.

In 1834, the church, as a means of redeeming itself from chaos and confusion, had adopted a set of " Rules," divided into " First Class " and " Second Class." They were partly religious, partly ecclesiastical, and partly parliamentary. These were found not to accomplish their object, but rather to render the members punctiliously captious. They were taken in hand and referred to a committee July 6, 1837, and after repeated efforts to amend them, they were finally, April 15, 1840, " suspended "— in which state they have continued till the present time. The moderator has found the application of the general principles of parliamentary practice acceptable to the church, and without fail successful in preserving order in all its ecclesiastical proceedings. It was among the things said to the present pastor by his cabinet at their first meeting after his installation, " We want a LEADER : the church wants *a moderator that has an opinion of his own.*" Such are indeed the conditions of prosperity in every church. But, alas, that in this case, the lips that uttered this language should be the first to take exception to these traits of character in the pastor. Principles whose excellence we celebrate when they operate in our aid, have not lost their abstract qualities when they are against us.

The ministry of Mr. Walker was the period of protracted meetings, and of that style of revivals that attends upon them. And although the present pastorate began in what may be called the reactionary period, there was yet a good degree of religious interest ; and in the year 1836, there were ten added to the church by profession, and in the year 1837, thirty-four. The fall and early winter of 1841 were remarkable for a spirit of prayer in the church ; and in the winter the answer came in the fullness of the blessing. January 17th there commenced a series of daily meetings that continued for three weeks,—not as a means of producing a revival, but as a demand of the public heart. The windows of heaven were open above us, and we could not refrain from meeting day by day, to receive the rich gifts that God was so freely bestowing. During the first week three services were held each day ; during the second week, two ; and during the third, an evening service only. The effect upon the community was, of course, great. The year that had its commencement in such glory, continued to be glorious. As the revival at its commencement was calm and rational, it could in its nature last. And it did last. There was at no time a rush ; but during this and the following year one hundred and ten were added to the church ; many of them persons in middle life, and not a few husbands and wives side by side.

It seemed, for a time, as if this elevated position of the church, now attained and so long occupied, was to be its permanent abode. But alas! it was too much for Satan to endure; and we, by and by, had experience of his power to prevent it. In immediate succession to this page of glory, must be written one of the most melancholy chapters to be found in the history of this or any other church ;—all the more dark to the eye of Christian tenderness, from its proximity to the brightness that had gone before it.

But must this chapter be written ? Were it not better to bury its melancholy facts in the deep gulf of oblivion, and save the credit thus of our holy religion ?

The motto of the historian is TRUTH ; and his one inquiry is, What is the " reality of things ? " For the consequences of the faithful record of the truth, he abjures all responsibility. God and the actors will bear that. So thought and acted the sacred historians. Our philosophy of expediency might have thought it best not to record the sin of Moses and of David and of Peter. And so of many of the dark chapters of Israel's history. The plan of Jehovah which embraced the facts, embraced also a record of the same. " Even so, Father, for so it seemeth good in thy sight." And perhaps even we can see some reasons why, for Christ's sake who is to save the world, a faithful record of the world should be preserved. With the historian's motto in our eye, then, we proceed to our solemn work.

At a church meeting held November 11, 1841, the subject of using alcoholic wine at the Lord's Supper was brought before the church. After some discussion, the subject was referred for consideration to an adjourned meeting. December 16th, at a meeting of the church, the following note addressed to the pastor was by him read:

"Dear Sir:—At a meeting of the New Ipswich Total Abstinence Society, the following Resolution was passed, with a vote that a copy of the same be transmitted to the clerks of both Religious Societies in this place,—viz.:

Resolved, That it is inconsistent with Total Abstinence principles to use Alcoholic Wine under any circumstances except as a medicine; and that we recommend the churches in this place to discontinue its use at the communion."

Without criticism upon the taste or propriety of this communication, it was laid upon the table, to be taken up with the general subject now on the docket.

At the Quarterly Meeting, July 7, 1842, the subject was considered; and it was "voted that a committee of three be chosen to report on the subject at a subsequent meeting." This committee, transcending their instructions, procured a few bottles of such sirup—the inspissated juice of the grape—as some churches had a few years before used. At the next Quarterly meeting (October 5) this committee reported "that they had procured a case of the unfermented sirup, and were in favor of the use of it." The church did not adopt this report, but "Voted that what has been procured, be used,"—by which was meant that only this be used; and that the church will, after, procure the pure wine that we had been informed could be now obtained. Accordingly, the agent of the church to spread the table, when this was gone, again used wine. This brought the subject again before the church. At its Quarterly Meeting, in January, 1844, the discussion was warm, and the matter again referred to a committee. And such was the state of feeling that the church "voted to observe Tuesday next as a season of fasting and prayer, and that a public meeting be held in this [the meeting] house at 2 o'clock, P. M."

The last named committee made a report, February 13, in favor of the use of the unfermented sirup. The motion to adopt was discussed for more than two hours, and finally laid on the table.

At a church meeting, April 4th, the subject was resumed, and finally and emphatically disposed of. It was "voted that wine be used at the communion," yeas 41, nays 4. It was also "voted that the opinions of the sisters be taken"—which was done. In favor of wine, 43; against it, 0. 41÷43=84 yeas; 4 nays.

In strict ecclesiastical propriety, the above vote was uncalled for. The common law of the church for eighteen hundred years had been interrupted by special legislation for a limited time. When that period had expired, the "common law" was again in force. The vote was put in that form in deference to the wishes of a venerable father in the church—the senior deacon—who, at a previous communion, had refused the cup, on the ground that there was no law of the church authorizing the administration of wine.

But while the wine question was, by the above vote, laid to rest ecclesiastically, the moral elements involved in it were never in a higher state of effervescence. And this department of our subject demands historic notice. May the motto of the historian guide the pen, through the special aid of the spirit of God.

This matter of sacramental reform had its origin and almost exclusive advocacy in a single family. A deacon, his son, and two sons-in-law, were the responsible agents. One of these sons-in-law was a son of another deacon, who, by this connection, was drawn into the party. The style of measures by and by became such as was uncongenial to the Christian and manly spirit of one of the sons-in-law, and he withdrew. The party then consisted of the two senior deacons of the church and a son each.

These two officers had stood in the same relation of seniority for many years. During the pastorate of the amiable and diffident Walker, they had held the reins of ecclesiastical administration in absolute sway, even to more than satisfaction. At any rate, they wanted more aid in the discharge of this duty. I do not impute this sway to them as a fault. It seemed a necessity. I know not how they could have done otherwise than take this responsibility. Still, the habit of rule had become a part of their condition and character. And when afterwards this necessity no longer existed, the habit remained.

The part which these officers of the church have acted in its affairs, renders proper a brief description of them. They were both Christians,— men who had been born again,—but were constitutionally and in their character and conduct very unlike.

The senior deacon was a man of strong mind, and quiet in its operations. He had only the very limited common education of his day, and while he read his Bible and had been taught his catechism, he was not familiar with books. But though he knew not the rules of the logic of the schools, he had logic in the sphere of common sense. He was affectionate, and of a loving spirit. He was modest and retiring. And while, for the best of reasons, he had confidence in his own opinions, and was firm, he was yet at the widest remove from ostentation or forwardness. And all these natural traits were sanctified and hallowed by the religion that for so many years had dwelt in his heart. It is due to him to say, that he belonged to a family in which insanity was an hereditary trait; especially in old age.

Possessed of such a character, he must, of course, have the respect and the love of his church. And his pastor loved and confided in him as he never loved and confided in any other man. In all emergencies, he went to him for counsel, as a son goes to a wise and good father.

At the period of which we are now speaking, he was an old man. The effects of age were very perceptible. The severity of the trial to which his mind and heart were subjected was more than he could bear. The sources of melancholy influence were *very near* him. When first overcome, his heart and mind could perceive it, and he retraced his steps. But that power, by and by, was gone. He seemed as in a labyrinth from which he could not extricate himself. His hereditary liability developed itself, and he died bereft of reason. He died a victim to the Wine Question—mourned and wept for by the man whom most he had injured, and who loves to think he shall meet him in a world where all his misapprehensions will be corrected, and more than the harmony and love of former years be renewed between them.

The last interview between the parties will never be forgotten by the survivor. He was, at the time, a member of the Legislature, and absent during the week. Returning on Saturday, he visited him, and found him near his end. When first he entered the room, the sick man turned upon him a wild and forbidding look, and did not give him the right hand of recognition. His wife proposed that his pastor should lead them in prayer. The prayer was from a heart that loved the burden it bore to the mercy-seat—that had the fullest confidence in the Christian character of the sick man, and could and did commend him in perfect assurance to the promised grace of the Savior. The answer was instant. The reason of the sufferer seemed in a good degree restored. The expression of the eye was changed to that of mildness and affection. He extended to his pastor a cordial hand, and they parted tenderly, and it is believed reconciled.

His immediate junior in office was all unlike him. Two
men more dissimilar could hardly be found. Though possessed of fair natural abilities, neither mind or heart were
much disciplined. Illogical, especially if in the least degree
excited, his opinions were entitled to little weight with the
considerate and judicious. And he was excitable in an
eminent degree. And, too, it was a marked feature in his
character, that the intellectual aberration produced by this
excitement did not come to an end with its cause. And
as he was pre-eminently ambitious, his highest excitements
were produced by any opposition to this his ruling passion.
And the type which, by a natural order of things, his
spirit would assume under the excitement of wounded
pride, was a gloomy hypochondria. This sometimes went
to such excess that his family and friends were alarmed
for his safety. All these constitutional infirmities were
held in check, of course, by religious principle. From
these traits of character it is evident that, while things
went smoothly, he would be an earnest and efficient executor in any sphere of agency. Such he was in the church.
The Sabbath School owes more to him than to any other
man. His place at the prayer meeting was seldom vacant.
He labored and did good in every method. This was especially true during Mr. Walker's ministry. Mr. Walker
was just the man with whom for him to co-operate.

But we may also infer that he would be an excited and
bitter antagonist; and if in the wrong, that he would be
difficult of reclamation. Once committed, he would be
persistent.

But what is there that grace cannot do? An answer is
found in the following anecdote: After years of distance,
during which the kindest "Good morning, Deacon," a
hundred times repeated, had been responded to, if at all,
by the coldest and slightest nod, he, one pleasant winter
morning, not long before his death, as he met his former

pastor in the street, came up to him and reached out the cordial hand, and said, " Good morning, Mr. Lee; I wish you a happy new year!" That pastor, with a heart that in an instant buried all the past and gushed out in the love of former years, said, " Good morning, Deacon, I wish you—I will not say a great many, for you are an old man, but I will say a good many happy new years." This, in tone and look and renewed grasp of the hand, was emphatically responded to. When, I say, such a scene as this occurred, how did it evince the triumphs of grace over our infirmities. And when, not long after, the paralytic stroke hushed the activities of the good man in the stillness of death, this new year's salutation was a pearl of great price.

Such were the men whose agency was most prominent in the sad events, the history of which we are now writing. As we have said, theirs had been the leadership of the church during the pastorate of Mr. Walker. They had acquired the *habit* of having things their own way—to an extent, indeed, of which themselves were not aware. And when they had introduced to the church the proposition for innovation upon the method of administering the sacrament, and expressed their preference for the same, it seemed to them but *right* that the pastor and almost the entire church should yield their preferences and even conscientious convictions. And they did most seriously urge upon the pastor and the church this concession. And they evinced their deep earnestness, by the amazing motive with which the duty was enforced—a regard on our part to " *the unity of the church !* "

It was in accordance with this extreme position, that all their measures were adopted. We have said, that after the sirup that had, by mistake, been procured, was all used, the sacrament was administered in the use of wine. After it had been twice used, these deacons consulted together, and decided on refusing the cup at the next communion—which they did, as did also their sons. This was the first Sabbath in March. On the 13th of February preceding, the church had spent an afternoon in the discussion of the subject, and had refused to obtain more of the sirup. The measure, therefore, of refusing the cup was *revolutionary*.

At this juncture, the pastor thought the time had come for the Bible to speak out on the subject; and on the 31st of March, he. preached what he had tried to make a thoroughly elaborated and exhaustive Scriptural argument for the use of wine at the communion. It is believed that it did its work. So far as is known, from that day to this, no member of the church has offered one word in advocacy of the innovation contemplated. True, at the meeting on the 4th of April, four *votes* were given against the use of wine. But votes are not always the true exponent of the heart.

Much has been said of this discussion of the subject from the pulpit—both the fact and the manner of the discussion. The pastor was told, in so many words, that he "had no right," when the church was considering such a question as that propounded by the innovators, to say any thing on the subject; and was threatened, if he did, he "would lose his best friends." The pastor could not concede this; and acted accordingly. It was a Bible subject, and belonged to his professional duty as the religious teacher of the church.

The *manner* was objected to as exceptionable. On this point the pastor has only to say that he has now at this writing, after the lapse of more than sixteen years, carefully read the sermon, and is ready to stand by every word of it. That the innovators should feel it to be a heavy burden is not unnatural. It was such, and was designed to be such. It was such because it was truth; and all the heavier in proportion as the argument was demonstrative, and the spirit of it kind and Christian.

But with the disposition of the wine question, the troubles of the church, from the same source as before, were not at an end. Defeated on this issue, *reprisals* were the next object. The minister must be dismissed.

The pastor had been told from the outset by the advocates of innovation, that for him to exert his influence against them would be dangerous; and now the threat was to be carried into effect.

At a meeting of the Committee of Examination at the pastor's study, August 8th, the senior deacons advised him to take a dismission. September 17th, the junior son gave the same advice. His reasons were, "You have carried every measure, and we have been defeated at every point; and I should think you could afford to step aside." And again—I repeat his very words—"A man of less talent and less influence would be more useful here in the circumstances"! The senior son had—in his own characteristic methods of ambiguity, of course, but very positively —taken the same position and avowed the same purpose, even before the final vote on the wine question.

But how could the pastor's dismission be effected? This was a question of difficult solution. The men who were now asking it had sat under his ministrations for eight years; and all this time they had bestowed upon him the highest praise—upon his personal character, his manner as a preacher, and his orthodoxy. It could not be charged that he had changed in any of these particulars. What, then, could be done?

First, the pastor was accused of excessive influence in the church. And there were men who could be affected by this argument. Such were systematically visited, and told how little influence they had, and how the pastor controlled every thing. Said a good man to his pastor,—and his manner and spirit were respectful and kind,—"I want to tell you, Mr. Lee, why I think you had better be dis-

missed. *Your influence is so great!* If you get up in a
church meeting and talk, it has more effect than if twenty
such men as I should express our mind." This reason
was, to him, entirely satisfactory.

The pastor was also accused—strange as it may seem—
of heresy. This was a difficult point to sustain by men
who had approved of his preaching for so many years, and
before a church who had heard with their own ears. But
nothing is too obviously false or too monstrous to be believed, if boldly asserted and repeated times enough. The
question of orthodoxy was a wide one, and could entertain
all sorts of operations. Particular phrases taken out of
their connection were repeated—as the thief quoted Scripture for his practice, "Let him that stole, steal. . . . . "
The preacher was made responsible for the illogical infer-
ences of others, &c., &c. This charge of heresy, however,
was the more embarrassing to those who were finally compelled to resort to it, from the fact that at the outset they
took special pains to disavow this. They said expressly
they had nothing of the serious kind to say against the
pastor—nothing against his Christian or ministerial character; it was solely his course on the wine question. This
cry of heresy has continued from 1844 to the present time.

Another argument openly urged by the disaffected was,
that they did not love their pastor, and he could not,
therefore, do them any good—an argument that would
justify, alas! how many in our world, in the attempt to
dethrone the Almighty.

Among the means employed, one was *contagion.* One
man, angry at his pastor, would talk and talk to another
of a certain temperament till he would catch the disease.

Another was *annoyance.* For instance: a poor, ignor-
ant man, that scarcely knew better, was encouraged in
going into the third meeting on the Sabbath, and making

stupid criticisms upon the sermons of the day. This was practiced and persisted in for a long time.

And—as man lives by bread, if not by bread alone,—the attempt was made to starve out the pastor by withholding support. This practice presented for the consideration of the church a very grave question, and that involved a vital principle. Fortunately, the church had been sound and avowed on the point for many years. In the days of Mr. Barbour, a debt was contracted by the church, in the purchase of his house—a debt which the sale of the house did not liquidate. To raise the necessary money, a committee, of which Dea. Clark was chairman, reported in favor of " an equitable assessment upon the members of the church, according to their respective polls and ratable estates," which was adopted. (Records, May 7, 1827.) During Mr. Walker's ministry, one hundred dollars of his annual salary was raised by the church as such, and on the same principle. (Records, June 4, 1828.)

The church now took the same ground. It avowed the doctrine that the church is a corporation, and in its corporate capacity is responsible for the support of the institutions of religion ; and that, therefore, the several members are responsible and amenable to the body for a tax assessed on the principle of "relative ability." The effort to "starve out," therefore, did not succeed.

I name one other. means, viz., slander and falsehood. Stories *without number* have been circulated, which their originators must have known were false—the veriest fabrications. But enough in this sort.

Among the means which the church resorted to in the hope of a more peaceful state, was the advice of an Ecclesiastical Council in two instances. The first was in November, 1846. This Council hoped to bring us peace by urging the methods of mildness. The fact was, the mildness of the church in presenting the case, misled their advisers, as themselves afterwards saw and said. The Council, however, commended the principles on which the church had proceeded, and advised to the exercise of discipline, if softer measures were without avail.

In accordance withthe spirit of this Result of Council, the church appointed a committee of eight to confer with the disaffected, and attempt a reconciliation. This committee, after earnest efforts to accomplish their object, presented, February 2, 1847, their report, from which the following is an extract :

" In regard to our venerated Brothers [the Senior Deacons] your committee would observe, that they have sought with strong and earnest solicitude for their reconciliation and ready Christian co-operation with the Pastor and church, in all the sacred, appropriate duties devolving upon them, which in their present station may be considered greatly conducive to the peace, the unity and the prosperity of the church. But we fear we have sought and labored in vain. If they still continue to entertain unfriendly and opposing views and feelings, they will readily perceive the propriety of retiring from their present *official station* in the church, and allow the same to be occupied by others of more congenial views and feelings."

This report, from the pen of the venerable chairman, Joseph Barrett, Esq., was presented as the unanimous opinion of the committee.

It was adopted by the church. But after some remarks by the loved men referred to in the above extract, the vote of adoption was reconsidered ; and the hope was indulged that there might yet be a reconciliation effected. The report was recommitted, with instructions to renew the efforts for peace. These efforts were made, and prolonged, but all was in vain. And the disease, uncured, unmitigated even, by every remedy, waxed worse and worse.

The other Council was in April, 1851. The design of the church was to lay the whole case before this Council, and abide its result. The disaffected gathered up all their charges against the church and pastor. The church had brought charges against certain of the disaffected, and, instead of adjudicating upon them themselves, submitted them to the Council. The Council was occupied three days with charges against the pastor. A majority of them could stay no longer. They advised the church and pastor, through a committee, to let go the charges against the disaffected. But the pastor and committee of the church utterly refused; and gave as a reason that the charges to be brought were of the most serious kind ; that the accused had forfeited their right to a place in the church of Christ, and they could not let the case pass by. The committee of Council, in reply, said, that what the church most of all needed was to "get rid" of these disturbers of her peace, and if the case should go to Council with these men unimpeached, and therefore in regular standing, the Council would recommend their dismission to other churches. The pastor still objected that his own defence in great part remained to be made through the witnesses that were to come in the trial of these accused members. The chairman of the committee (Dr. Whiton) assured him that he was in no need of such defence, as his character never stood so high in the eye of his brethren as at that hour. Still the pastor and committee refused to withdraw their well considered charges against the men whose offences had risen up to heaven. At a subsequent interview with the pastor and committee, the committee of Council informed them that there was a *necessity* in the case : the Council could not remain longer in session, i. e. a majority of them. Necessity, of course, prevails. But alas! for the church, that a work so essential to its own peace and the honor of religion should not have been done!

The Council then say of the pastor, "There is nothing sustained in the complaints which impairs their confidence in his Christian or ministerial character."

They advise the dismission and recommendation of the disaffected, who may request it, and prescribe a form of certificate to the clerk.

Of the church, they say, "The Council are happy to witness the mutual confidence which exists between this beloved church and pastor, and hope, by the blessing of God, they may edify one another, and build up the kingdom of Christ among them."

The disaffected then took their letters and went, some to one church and some to another. Most of them went to the Congregational Church in Mason Village, by which they received a not welcome reception,—the pastor expressing to them his regret that they should apply for admission.

October 9th of this same year, a Second Congregational Church was organized, in New Ipswich, made up chiefly of members who retired from this. The agitations of the time had effected a separation in the church on a principle in morals like, and scarcely less rigid and uniform than that of material particles of different specific gravities when shaken. The law of elective affinity in chemistry is scarcely more noticeable than in this moral process. Each church is composed of congenial spirits—with some exceptions, of course, from peculiar circumstances.

The organization of a Second Congregational Church in this town was felt to be, in itself, undesirable. There was no more population than could be accommodated in one congregation. And besides, there was not wealth sufficient to sustain two organizations.

But it was regarded as the least of two evils. For more than the quarter of a century this church had been in a broil. Two ministers had been cruelly treated and driven from their pulpits. And the very men who were now attempting the dismission of the pastor had been the chief agents in their dismission. The church thought the time had come to take a stand.

The church claimed that majorities have rights, and that this large church, so much attached to their minister, were permitted of right, and ought of principle, to stand by themselves and him. And if a few in the church could not love a minister who had more influence than themselves, that few, and not the church, were responsible for the fact, and must meet the consequences of extreme measures. And they determined to stand by their pastor, and their pastor determined to stand by them. And they have done it, and lost a part of their number.

But so far from any consciousness of weakness from the separation, they had never before felt so strong. The church and society were now a united agency ; and union is strength. There was more than strength;—there was a joyous elasticity such as the present generation had never known. This was evinced in their enterprises, the chief of which was the remodeling of their meeting-house—a work that never could have been done with all the discordant elements together. This beautiful and convenient house is an effect of the division.

A reference to the pastor's receipt-book would show the same fact. A new style of punctuality in the payment of his salary was then inaugurated.

So of our church meetings. Their records, how unlike the record of the twenty-five years preceding! Yes, with us subtraction was addition ; loss was gain ; adversity was prosperity.

But though our disaffected members had gone out from us, and were no longer of us, they did not abandon their supreme object. They have labored just as pertinaciously as before, both at home and abroad, to effect the one great object in which would consist their victory over the mother church—the dismission of its minister. We have been unable to see that there is not as close and careful attention paid to him, and as many fabrications to the prejudice of his character, as when we were all of the same church. And these efforts are, of course, not without effect. There are, in all communities, minds that will be influenced by such a "continual dropping in a very rainy day." Some are over-credulous, some are wanting in moral courage, and some, by a change of circumstances, experience a change in collateral motives.

But all has been in vain ; and the principles for the support of which this church and society with its pastor took their stand, they have maintained unto the end. The church and congregation have stood by their pastor, and he has stood by them till his work is done. And all this expensive effort—this sacrifice of more than sixteen years of precious time—of the lives, literally, of some who, but for this cause, might probably have been with us to-day— of so much treasure wrung from the purses of poor men, some of whom have cheated their creditors in consequence —of so much of agony by day and by night—of so much slander, and defamation, and malice, and wrath, and evil-speaking,—of all the dishonor brought upon our holy religion, and all this riveting of the chains of sin upon unconverted men,—of all the chagrin and mortification of the principal actors, with the disgrace which they have brought upon themselves and their families,—*all* have been in vain. And the enterprise to which all these costly sacrifices have been offered, has proved an UTTER FAILURE.

And this venerable church, in its solemn stand for principles and for God—the principles and the God of our fathers—has, through the grace and the good providence of God, achieved *a perfect victory.* The triumph in its completeness is realized to-day. God of our fathers, we praise Thee, and confide to the God of the Past, our successors of the coming century.

After the division, the church moved on peacefully, and with little of special interest to the pen of the historian. In the winter of 1853–4, the health of the pastor declined, and the summer following he spent at Saratoga, and did not resume his labors till October. In the winter of 1857 –8 was an interesting revival, as the fruits of which fifteen united with the church the following season; while a much greater number, members of the Academy, and whose homes were away, were the hopeful subjects of the work.

At a meeting of the church, held the 5th of April last, it was "voted, that as the present is the one hundredth year since the organization of this church, we will celebrate this Centennial Anniversary,"—and a committee of arrangements was accordingly chosen.

During the past season, much has been said of a union of the two Congregational churches in this place. Members of the Second Church had repeatedly urged the subject upon the attention of members of our own body, and had claimed that the initiative was not of propriety theirs, but ours. Although differing from them in opinion on this point, we were not disposed to quarrel on a question of etiquette; and at a meeting of the church, held August 12th, it was

" Resolved, That we are ready to respond in Christian charity and love to any action of the Second Congregational Church in New Ipswich, which shall contemplate a union of that church with us, on any conditions which shall not disturb our relations to our present pastor."

The Second Church respond to this as follows :

" Whereas, the First Congregational Church in this place have expressed to us their readiness, under certain conditions, to respond in Christian charity and love to any action on our part, which shall contemplate a union of the two churches; therefore,

Resolved, That we cordially respond to this expression of brotherly love, and hold ourselves in readiness to meet with them for unrestricted conference upon the subject of a union, either by a committee or otherwise, at any time they may select."

To this we reply as follows:

" Whereas, our brethren of the Second Church cordially accept our proposal to discuss the question of a union of the two churches under the conditions specified by us, and are ready by a committee to meet a committee that may be chosen by us; therefore,

Voted, that we will appoint a committee of conference to consist of five,"—which was done.

The Second Church then signify their non-acceptance of our proposal thus:

" Whereas, when proposing to appoint a committee of conference upon the subject of union of the two churches in this place, we did not deem it consistent with good faith on our part to interpose any conditions of conference, and therefore did not accept, nor profess to accept, any such conditions; and

Whereas, our brethren of the First Church, having misunderstood our previous action, have stated upon their records that we did accept such conditions, and have appointed a committee upon the basis of that misunderstanding; therefore,

Resolved, That as we cannot, in justice to ourselves, or with adherence to truth, take any steps to meet their committee while their records thus misrepresent our action, we do hereby, in all brotherly kindness, earnestly request them to rescind and expunge from their records the statement that we accepted their proposal to discuss the question of union under the conditions specified by them; also,

Resolved, That we choose a committee of five for unrestricted conference upon the subject of the union of the two churches, which shall hold themselves in readiness to meet any committee chosen by the First Church, upon the same basis, at any time they may appoint."

On receipt of this, the church voted the indefinite postponement of the whole subject.

The new century, then, comes in to witness two Congregational churches in New Ipswich.

One word, in conclusion, of general statistics. Since

the organization of this church, there is the record of the admission of one thousand one hundred and seventy-eight, of which by profession nine hundred and eighty-nine, by letter one hundred and eighty-nine. If but twenty-two be added to the total, it will be one thousand two hundred. More than this number must have been admitted during the period left blank in our records. In round numbers, then, we may say, the members of this church have been one thousand two hundred,—by letter two hundred, by profession one thousand,—an average of one each month.

Thus have we completed the history of the first hundred years of this church. This history cannot be surpassed in interest and importance by the history of any other century. The beginnings of things are important. They are the germ and the first growth. And the future is of necessity shaped by it. We that are living, are what we are from the circumstances of our birth and education and life as they were determined for us by our predecessors. They were more emphatically of the germinant state than ourselves; yet as compared with the indefinite future that stretches itself out before us, we are inceptive, and the responsibilities of beginners are shared largely by us with our fathers.

Standing on this solemn point, between a century past— a first century, and the centuries, of indefinite number, of the future, we may well survey the past and look out upon what is to come.

The former we have done. And we ought to learn from that past lessons of wisdom to be applied to duties that await us. In the history of this church we have the history of good men, christian men, men who revered the

Bible and the Sabbath and the Pulpit, men of prayer and who communed with God, men of principle and who stood by their principles at great cost. They should be our example. And they should be our encouragement. That such men have gone before us implies that our surroundings, as inherited, are favorable to virtue,—its existence and growth, and also its conquests and extension. That such men have lived and prayed, upon these hills and in these valleys, implies a favoring purpose in heaven towards us their successors. Availability in our behalf before the mercy seat is laid up and in waiting.

But there are evils to deplore from which we should also learn the lessons of wisdom. It has been the misfortune of this church of good, praying and self-denying men and women, to suffer in reputation by the imputation to them of the sins of other and different men. This church has had the reputation, for at least the last third of the century, of being quarrelsome and factious. It has quarreled with, and abused, and literally killed some of its ministers. Mr. Walker was killed by the treatment he received when here. His tender heart was broken, and he went away, like a " stricken deer " to bleed and die. And his successor, so unlike him, has not with a single arrow infixed, fled, but has stood for about three-fourths of his quarter of a century, with his flesh full of arrows, barbed, poisoned, rankling;—stood in agony, but stood, and stands to-day, and till his work is done. But such wounds of course are mortal. And his end will be an effect from the same cause that crushed his predecessor into his grave.

But *the church* has not done this, and is responsible for it only indirectly. The real positive actors have been few. In Mr. Walker's day how few were the agitators. Indeed but for one solitary pertinacious disturber, there would have been peace, and that good man might probably have lived and preached to and blessed this people till the present day, and written for this centennial a history of the church, how unlike the present!

So in this eighteen years' war, the smoke of which is in our nostrils to-day. It originated in some three or four, and has been perpetuated by a leadership of even smaller number.

The lesson we are to learn from these facts is, that we are to "mark those who cause divisions, and have no fellowship with them." The observation of thirty years of pastoral life has taught me to have little confidence in the men who are inclined to create parties in the church. A quarrelsome Christian is a contradiction in terms.

Again, the history of this church has taught me that the principle of *rotation in office* should be applied to the church. Congregationalism is essentially democracy—a government by the people. The administration of the affairs of the church is by the church. Let them share among themselves the responsibilities, and if there are honors, the honors also of such administration. The evils of a permanent deaconship and committeeship are not few. It keeps many from that degree of responsibility and prominence that are essential to the best development of character. It denies the pastor the opportunity, that would else be furnished, to become thoroughly acquainted with his church. He should meet and confer with them in larger numbers in the committee-room. It has a tendency to inflate and invest with inordinate self-importance the men who hold office. Give a man with office also a crushing weight of responsibility, and make him amenable to and dependent for his daily bread upon his supporters, and he will be apt to be humble. But take a man of only ordinary education and information, and elevate him from his equals by an office and a name and honor, and with no dependence, and all this for life, and he becomes—this is the rule rather than the exception—of great consequence

K

in his own eyes, and in such degree that usefulness is not the prominent characteristic of the man. There is not one man in five that is not liable to be spoiled by the office and the name, as permanent, of deacon. Nothing can be more obvious and certain than that it is to the effect of this cause that we are to ascribe all our troubles of the last eighteen years, and the existence, so uncalled for, of a Second Church. And I have had extensive acquaintance with troubles in other churches; and most of them have had their origin in the self-consequence of the officers of the church. Now rotation in office would correct all this. And I do now, as among the last things which I expect to say to this church that I have so long served, and so tenderly love, advise them to adopt this principle. And it may be remarked that the present is a favorable time for the change. Were the men in office less worthy of our confidence there would be more delicacy attending it, and a greater liability to the suspicion of personality. You can now do it on principle.

Again, one of the lessons we are to learn from the past century is, not to be discouraged by difficulties. The history of this church is a history of difficulties and of successes in close connection, and often in union. This is especially true of the last half of the century. All the quarrels with ministers, and all the outbreaks of faction have been in this period; and, save one, all the revivals. No period has been more stormy than Mr. Walker's, and never more frequent revivals. Even that time of glory—the winter of 1841–2—was during the incipient effervescence of the wine question; and the most furious outbreak of the troubles on that subject was into the midst of the blessed and peaceful results of that revival.

In the Apocalypse, (chap. xx,) we are informed that just before the coming in of the glory of the consummated kingdom of Christ on earth, Satan, as a persecutor, will

be let loose for a little season. This is just what philosophy would predict. The success of religion provokes the
Devil. And we must expect he will employ the weaknesses
of very partially sanctified Christians, and especially the
selfishness of unconverted men in the church, to injure
the cause of Christ ; and that these classes of men will be
incited and active for evil, in proportion as religious success provokes the adversary. Let not the church, then,
be discouraged by the storms she has to meet. The plants
of righteousness will grow all the more when the sun
shall shine. Such are the lessons from the past.

But we are to turn from the past, and from this same
high stand-point of observation look out upon the future.
Among the influences which God has made to bear upon
the character and conduct of his people, is a knowledge,
more or less distinct, of the future. And He has addressed
their hopes, rather than their fears, by the page of prophecy.
And facts of the past and the present are prophetic, no
less than the voice of the seer. Both prophecy and facts
are significant to the men of our day.

We may reasonably suppose that one hundred years
from this day, our posterity will meet and listen to the
history of the church. They will epitomize the period
over which we have passed, and then, more in detail, recall
the facts of a century.

What shall that history be ? First on the record will
be the fact that the pastor who had served the church for
nearly a quarter of a century, weary and worn, laid off his
armor, yearning for rest ; and that the church, as they
entered upon a new century, were called to choose a new
pastor. May it be said of him that shall succeed, that he
was a good man and full of the Holy Ghost ; that he was
learned in all the wisdom of this day of light ; and especially that he read and interpreted for himself God's Bible ;
that he was tender and kind and gentle, but fearless, not

not shunning to declare the whole counsel of God; that he was progressive—ready to absorb the light that God may give to the diligent and earnest and independent seeker; and that his labor was not in vain in the Lord.

But what else? We know only in general. That it is to be a history of grace and glory begun on earth, we hope and believe. Not immediately, however. There are elements of evil in the present, that God's providence must slowly remove—how slowly, and by what methods, of course we know not. But a purer church shall pray and labor and be blessed of God here. Another style of piety shall be developed. Its germination and incipient stages of development are now very obvious. The change in the type of personal religion noticeable in this church since the writer has been an observer of its history, is the great fact for which he is most thankful to the God of our successes. Begun, it shall progress, and its course shall be onward and onward still, to its consummation. It is among the hopeful indications of the present day, that the piety of the church very generally, not less than formerly the piety of principle, has yet a more adequate and practical conception of what are the privileges of the sons of God—what the exceeding riches of the grace of God in Christ Jesus. It fears not less, but loves more.

This process in the church will be attended by a corresponding process out of the church. Religion will be seen more as it is, and commend itself with a more resistless power to the acceptance of men. It will address, not in undue proportion the fears of men, but also their hopes, and their conscious capabilities throughout. And revivals of pentecostal and more than pentecostal power will occur. Nor shall they be local, but spread themselves out over whole and extended communities and the world.

And not the prospective history of religion alone gladdens our hearts, but of education, and of intellectual and social development; of science and the arts, and of their union in the most efficient practical bearing upon the state of society and of the very material world. What shall not the coming century witness? How near to its fulfilment will be the prediction that the tabernacle of God shall be with men, and the New Jerusalem come down from God out of heaven, and the throne of God and the Lamb be on earth, and the river of the water of life, clear as crystal, flow forth from beneath that throne to refresh and bless all nations!

Of course, we can give no definite answer to such an inquiry. But we know that moral changes, after a feeble inception and tardy growth for a season, do, with a certain attainment made, develop themselves suddenly and wonderfully to their consummation. When Isaiah, in vision, was contemplating the kingdom of the Messiah just at this stage, he exclaimed, "Shall a nation be born in a day!" We are approaching that point. The preparations for it of the last half century have been wonderful. The beauty of the blossom is maturing within. Suddenly its petals shall open, and that beauty stand disclosed.

> " How long, dear Savior, O how long
> Shall this bright hour delay?
> Fly swifter round, ye wheels of time,
> And bring the welcome day! "

I hope, more than hope, that this day shall be one of the century upon the threshold of which this church is now standing. Perhaps the child is born whose eyes shall behold and rest upon its glory.

But who shall tell this child of Christ? Who has such views of Christ and the riches of his grace and glory, that the child, accepting the Savior as by him presented, shall become the Christian for such a day?

THE CENTENNIAL CELEBRATION.

The Church was organized October 21. But this occurred Sabbath day the present year. The Celebration, therefore, was on Monday following,—one of the days of the session of the Council, and the day of the ordination of the Pastor.

The following is the programme prepared by the Committee:
1. Gathering at the site of the old meeting-house. Prayer and brief address, 10 A. M.
2. Procession to the Church.
3. Historical Discourse, 11 A. M.
4. Dinner in the basement of the Church, with Addresses.
5. Sacrament of the Lord's Supper in the Church.

A flag had been reared on the site of the FIRST meeting-house, on Farrar Hill, and which could be seen from the place of gathering. There are those living who remember the underpinning stones of that house, and can identify the spot.*

The Pastor was unable to deliver the Address. That part of it which relates to Mr. Farrar was read by Rev. Mr. Fisher of Mason Village; that including the ministries of Messrs. Hall, Barbour and Walker, by Rev. Mr. Bell of Ashby, and the remainder, by Rev. I. S. Perry of Bellows Falls, Vermont.

The following original Hymn was sung:

God of our favored Past,
    We glorify thy name,
Thy praise shall ever last,
    Thou ever art the same.

We thank Thee for this day
    Of sacred memories,
And on Thine altar lay,
    The tribute of our praise.

Thou wast our fathers' God,
    Their hope was all in Thee;
And onward firm they trod
    The path of destiny.

Unconscious of their day,
    They lived to make us blest;
Foundations deep to lay,
    On which for us to rest.

O, God, we give Thee praise
    For such illustrious sires;
And here our altars raise,
    And kindle now our fires.

Their God we worship too,
    Their Savior we adore;
Honored if we may do
    What they have done before;

Their service re-enact,
    Their spirit be our own;
And us the power attract,
    Which kept them near the throne.

Their service done below,
    They gain a rich reward;
So may we also know
    The glory of the Lord.

At the Dinner, the following Sentiments were propounded:
1. The Father of the New Ipswich Ministry. "The memory of the just is blessed." Responded to by the venerable Dr. Oliver Scripture, of Hollis,—since deceased.

* On a small plat ten rods S., 6° 30' E. from the highest point of the hill.

2. Rev. Richard Hall. He feared God, and God only. Response from Rev. Dr. Burnham of Rindge.

3. Rev. Charles Walker. Like David, he came from the sheep-cote; like him, he was of a tender and loving spirit. He was loved of the good and owned and blessed of God. Rev. Mr. Goodyear of Temple responded, and said he was the " Apostle John of the New Ipswich ministry."

4. The First Congregational Church, the mother of ministers. Responded to by Rev. I. S. Perry, one of her clerical sons. More than twenty of her sons have been ministers.

5. The First Congregational Church, the mother of missionaries. Rev. J. G. D. Stearns.

6. The First Congregational Church, the mother of a numerous seed, scattered over the length and breadth of our land, that honor their parent, and " stand up for Jesus." Rev. William Spaulding.

7. The Sabbath School—its relation to the Church, to Christ, and to the world. Charles Taylor, Superintendent of Sabbath School.

8. Our Academy—the worthy coadjutor of the Church. E. T. Quimby, Principal of Academy.

9. The new Century—full of hope. P. B. Davis, Theological Seminary, Andover.

The following correspondence, omitted in its proper place, may be inserted here.

Rev. Sam'l Lee,
Dear Sir:

At a meeting of the Church, Nov. 22, 1860, the following vote was passed:

Voted, That a copy of the Historical Address of the Pastor at our late Centennial Celebration, be requested for publication.

The subscribers were made a committee of publication.

Respectfully Yours,

GILMAN AMES,
NEWTON BROOKS,
CHAS. TAYLOR,
E. F. FOX,
J. U. DAVIS.

New Ipswich, Nov. 26, 1860.

Messrs. G. Ames, and others, " Committee of Publication."
Gentlemen:

I comply with your request, and send you the manuscript of my Discourse. It has imperfections which better health would have corrected. I have prepared it under the pressure of bodily infirmities, and chiefly by the use of the eyes and the pen of another. Still, it is a faithful record. And I have spared no pains to derive information from every available source. I submit it as a labor of love to posterity.

Very truly yours,   SAMUEL LEE.
Nov. 26, 1860.